WordPress Complete

A comprehensive, step-by-step guide on how to set up, customize, and market your blog using WordPress

Hasin Hayder

BIRMINGHAM - MUMBAI

WordPress Complete

First published: November 2006

Production Reference: 1161106

Published by Packt Publishing Ltd.
32 Lincoln Road
Olton
Birmingham, B27 6PA, UK.

ISBN 1-904811-89-2

www.packtpub.com

Cover Image by www.visionwt.com

Credits

Author

Hasin Hayder

Reviewer

Nikhil Bangera

Development Editor

Nanda Padmanabhan

Technical Editor

Priyanka Baruah

Editorial Manager

Dipali Chittar

Project Manager

Patricia Weir

Project Coordinator

Abhijeet Deobhakta

Indexer

Bhushan Pangaonkar

Proofreader

Chris Smith

Layouts and Illustrations

Shantanu Zagade

Cover Designer

Shantanu Zagade

About the Author

Hasin Hayder graduated in Civil Engineering from the Rajshahi University of Engineering and Technology (RUET) in Bangladesh. He is a Zend-certified Engineer and an expert in localization. Hasin is currently working in one of the leading Ajax startpage company Pageflakes Ltd (`www.pageflakes.com`) as a Development Engineer. He is also working in Somewhere In (`www.somewherein.net`) as a Web Application Developer. Hasin is an expert WordPress user and has developed several themes and plug-ins for the community. He also maintains the WordPress4SQLite project, which is an unofficial port of WordPress to be used with SQLite. You can reach Hasin at `hasin@somewherein.net` as well as at `hasin@pageflakes.com`. You can also visit Hasin's personal blog at `http://hasin.wordpress.com` when you are free.

First of all, I would like to thank David Barnes, Patricia Weir, Abhijeet Deobhakta, Nanda Padmanabhan, Nikhil Bangera, and Priyanka Baruah, without whom the book would have never seen the daylight. I would also like to thank Mohan Rapheal and Jimmy Karumalil for their efforts. After writing for so many sleepless nights, the book is finally over; but I want to thank all those who supported me at that time. My wife Ayesha for storytelling, Little Afif for missing his Papa, the staff of Somewhere In for receiving a sleepy developer in the morning, the staff of Pageflakes for their inspiration, and all the members of my PHP group, phpexperts. I would also like to thank all my family members for their great support during this period. Finally, I dedicate this book to the person who would have been the happiest person to see it; my father, Ali Akbar Mohammad Mohiuddin Hayder (1934-2006).

About the Reviewer

Nikhil Bangera graduated with a degree in Computer Science from Mumbai University and currently works as an Editor. His academic interests lie in Databases and Computer Security and he feels passionately about anything open source. This made him choose WordPress while looking for a platform to profess his obeisance to The Beatles.

I would like to thank my Mom and Dad for all their love and for keeping me with them for so long. To all my friends who love me, though I still show no promise of ever doing anything useful.

Table of Contents

Preface

WordPress is an open-source blog engine released under the GNU general public license. It allows users to easily create dynamic blogs with great content and many outstanding features. It is an ideal tool for developing blogs and though it is chiefly used for blogging, it can also be used as a complete CMS with very little effort. Its versality and ease of use have attracted a large, enthusiastic, and helpful community of users.

If you want to create powerful, fully featured blogs in no time, this book is for you. This book will help you explore WordPress showing you what it offers and how to go about building your blog with the system.

You will be introduced to the main aspects of a blog — users, communities, posts, comments, news feeds — and learn how to manage them using WordPress. You will develop the skills and confidence to manage all types of content, be it text or images, on your blog, and also understand how users interact with the blog. In working through the book you'll be inspired as well as informed, and have the capability and the ideas to make your blog cutting edge and exciting to maximize its impact.

What This Book Covers

Chapter 1 will take you to the world of blogging by introducing different blog engines available on the Internet. This chapter will also introduce you to the types of blog and the core parts of a blog. You will find this chapter very helpful to find out what the major blog engines are and why we choose WordPress among them.

In *Chapter 2,* you will learn how to start using WordPress as a blog engine. You can either register your blog at wordpress.com or set up in your own web host. You will learn how to install WordPress using FTP, how to manage permissions in the MySQL database, how to install it from cPanel, and how you can upgrade your old WordPress blog to a newer one. This chapter also shows the basic operations to kick start your blog.

One of the main attractive features of WordPress is the availability of thousands of themes. *Chapter 3* will guide you to where you can get best themes for your blog and how to choose from them. You will also learn basic modification of themes for a quick change in your blod's appearance.

Chapter 4 will guide you through the details of administering articles and comments in your blog. It will introduce you to all exciting features that may come handy while writing articles. This chapter also shows you how you can post remotely via using the MetaWeblog API and XML RPC interfaces.

Chapter 5 guides you through converting a WordPress blog into full fledged website by using its content management features. With a minimal level of coding you can use WordPress as an awesome content engine for any general purpose website. In this chapter we discuss this process step by step that you can understand it easily.

Delivering feeds and podcasts are what you will learn from *Chapter 6*. Using all these tricks you can use WordPress as a great tool for audio blogging. You can increase the traffic and quality of your blog by delivering RSS feeds. This chapter will guide you through all these features in a nice and readable way so that you can grasp it quickly.

Chapter 7 is one of the most exciting chapter in this book, which will teach you to develop awesome themes for WordPress. You don't need to be a PHP pro to write themes at all. This chapter will show you how you can add cool features to your WordPress theme with a minimal level of coding. This chapter will also introduce you to online theme generators, which will ease your life.

Blogging is for community and that is what you will learn from *Chapter 8*. How to turn your blog into a community blogging site and how to manager privileges among users is covered in this chapter.

Chapter 9 will introduce you to the world of plug-ins and widgets. You can extend the WordPress engine by using these plug-ins and widgets, add awesome features to your blog, and release them to community. This chapter will guide you through the detailed lifecycle of WordPress plug-ins, developing them and working with then cleverly with automated installations. This is one of the coolest chapter from this book.

Chapter 10 will describe all the administrative tasks of your WordPress blog. You will learn how to upgrade WordPress, how to trouble-shoot some installation and post installation errors, how to install WordPress MU, and how to back up and restore your blog. This is one of the most important chapters in this book, which you will want to read time and again.

Conventions

In this book, you will find a number of styles of text that distinguish between different kinds of information. Here are some examples of these styles, and an explanation of their meaning.

There are three styles for code. Code words in text are shown as follows: "We can include other contexts through the use of the `include` directive."

A block of code will be set as follows:

```php
<?php
// ** MySQL settings ** //
define('DB_NAME', 'WordPress');      // The name of the database
define('DB_USER', 'username');       // Your MySQL username
define('DB_PASSWORD', 'password');   // and password
```

When we wish to draw your attention to a particular part of a code block, the relevant lines or items will be made bold:

```php
<?php
// ** MySQL settings ** //
define('DB_NAME', 'WordPress');      // The name of the database
define('DB_USER', 'username');       // Your MySQL username
define('DB_PASSWORD', 'password');   // and password
```

Any command-line input and output is written as follows:

```
update wp_options set option_value='http://newdomain/wordpress'
where option_name='siteurl' and option_value='home'
```

New terms and **important words** are introduced in a bold-type font. Words that you see on the screen, in menus or dialog boxes for example, appear in our text like this: "Click on the **Delete** button from the upper-right portion of this page."

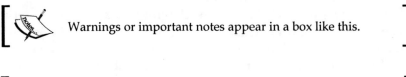

Warnings or important notes appear in a box like this.

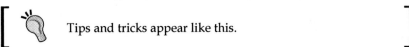

Tips and tricks appear like this.

Reader Feedback

Feedback from our readers is always welcome. Let us know what you think about this book, what you liked or may have disliked. Reader feedback is important for us to develop titles that you really get the most out of.

To send us general feedback, simply drop an email to feedback@packtpub.com, making sure to mention the book title in the subject of your message.

If there is a book that you need and would like to see us publish, please send us a note in the **SUGGEST A TITLE** form on www.packtpub.com or email suggest@packtpub.com.

If there is a topic that you have expertise in and you are interested in either writing or contributing to a book, see our author guide on www.packtpub.com/authors.

Customer Support

Now that you are the proud owner of a Packt book, we have a number of things to help you to get the most from your purchase.

Downloading the Example Code for the Book

Visit http://www.packtpub.com/support, and select this book from the list of titles to download any example code or extra resources for this book. The files available for download will then be displayed.

The downloadable files contain instructions on how to use them.

Errata

Although we have taken every care to ensure the accuracy of our contents, mistakes do happen. If you find a mistake in one of our books—maybe a mistake in text or code—we would be grateful if you would report this to us. By doing this you can save other readers from frustration, and help to improve subsequent versions of this book. If you find any errata, report them by visiting http://www.packtpub.com/support, selecting your book, clicking on the **Submit Errata** link, and entering the details of your errata. Once your errata have been verified, your submission will be accepted and the errata added to the list of existing errata. The existing errata can be viewed by selecting your title from http://www.packtpub.com/support.

Questions

You can contact us at questions@packtpub.com if you are having a problem with some aspect of the book, and we will do our best to address it.

1
WordPress and the World of Blogging

In the world of the Internet, you must have some sort of website to publish your identity. It could be somewhere where you can write about your work and interests. You may also write an online diary, which would be more interesting to read. People get to know you more than through any other media when they read about your regular activities, your thoughts, and news about you. These sorts of diaries are made for public viewing. People usually don't post their very personal or confidential information here.

These online diaries are interesting fields to grab news. "Netizens" describe these diaries with a special term "blog", which is actually derived from the word "weblog". Blogs are places where you make yourself global. They can be of different types. People always log news that interests them. Some write about music, some about politics, some about sports, and so forth. Blogs are the best place if you want to collect recent news. In real life when some natural disaster takes place or something special happens, journalists and other people always search these blogs to be up-to-date. Recently, after the tsunami or after the bombings in London, the very first news was published in blogs. Blogs are a world-renowned system for publishing your content; there are several million active bloggers in this world.

Blogging History

According to **Wikipedia**, the largest free encyclopedia, the term "**weblog**" was first used by John Barger in 1997. In May, 1999, Peter Merholz converted the word into a new term keeping the characters the same. He made it "we blog" instead of "weblog". He especially pointed out the term "blog". Shortly after that, this word was globally accepted both as a noun meaning a weblog and as a verb meaning "to post in someone's blog".

One of the early blog sites "**Xanga**" had 100 weblogs in 1997, which surprisingly turned into 50 million by the end of 2005. People started using blogs globally in 1999. Blogging started becoming popular when among others, Evan Williams and Meg Hourihan from Pyra Labs created their blog publishing tool **Blogger**. Using this site anyone can start blogging within minutes. The whole system was free and very attractive. Surprisingly, Google bought the whole service in 2004. Blogger is still a free blog-publishing tool, but under the banner of Google. The words "weblog", "weblogging", and "weblogger" were inserted into *The Oxford Dictionary* in March, 2003. This purely indicates the magic of the word "blog", which is still the favorite publishing system among millions of people.

By the end of 2001, blogging had become more popular. Everyone focused on the possibilities and importance of blogs. Shortly after that people started researching on blogging. Even schools of journalism were very interested in the whole process.

There are other publishing systems like Wikis and CMSs, which also gained popularity in the meantime. CMS stands for Content Management System and these are generally used for publishing articles, news content, or general content in a website. They are especially built for maintaining every kind of website. Joomla, CivicSpace, Typo3, and DotnetNuke are popular CMS software systems. There is also a special kind of CMS that is called a Wiki. In Wikis any user can modify contents, and all the posts are editable by general users; and usually, Wikis are devoted to a specific audience. A Wiki tracks every change made by the users so that you can find who changed the information and why. One of the most popular Wiki engines is MediaWiki (`http://www.mediawiki.com`). A blog is also a kind of content management system but the main purpose is to maintain the articles chronologically.

Anatomy of a Blog

Unlike blogs, a blog engine is not a single website. However, the engine consists of different parts that are organized in a very structured way. Let us first discuss what the different types of blogs are.

Types of Blogs

In the real world, there are different types of blogs. I do not actually mean their purpose, but rather the category of their contents. In the following sections, you will see some of them and understand their necessity.

General Blogs

When people say 'blog', they usually mean the blogs that belong to this category. These blogs are generally text-based, but contain a lot of images and other media like audio and video. These blogs are easy to maintain, lightweight, and are very popular for their simplicity. WordPress and Drupal are general blog engines.

Photo Blogs

Photoblogs or **Phlogs** are special kind of blogs where a group of people or individuals share their photos collected from various sources. These blogs are generally dedicated towards a specific audience. Most photoblogs are free. The usual subjects of photoblogs are films, wars, herbs, natural beauty or even weird images, and so forth; it's impossible to specify all of them. Professional photographers also share photos through their blogs.

In photoblogs, images are the main content; we all know that a picture speaks a thousand words. Among the photoblogs, one of the most important is `Photoblogs.org`, which is developed by Brandon Stone. Photoblogs.org started with 15 blogs in 2002 and now it contains around 10,000 blogs in 40 languages!

Some photobloggers upload images in their web space using any FTP application and directly link them through their blogs. Some bloggers use online photo repositories like Flickr (`www.flickr.com`), SmugMug (`http://www.smugmug.com/`), or Zoomr (`www.zoomr.com`) to reduce the bandwidth and also to achieve full-fledged image administration. These days PicasaWeb (`http://picasaweb.google.com/`) is also a very popular image-sharing service.

Mobile Blogs

Mobile blogs are often known as **Moblogs**. In this type of blogs, people access the contents and modify them for their mobile phones or portable devices like PDAs. Moblogs are usually developed in Japan where people have a huge number and variety of portable devices with cameras. The term Moblog was suggested by Adam Greenfield, who also arranged the First International Moblogging Conference (1IMC) in July, 2003. Mobile blogs are very popular these days due to the availability of portable devices. In 2004, on Singapore's national day, a **national Moblog** was launched, which is the first national moblog in the world. Mobile blogs are often known as gLogs (pronounced as glogs), when they are especially used as photoblogs.

Audio Blogs

Audio blogs are especially designed MP3 blogs, whose contents are downloadable in MP3 format. Most audio blogs are devoted to a special genre of music like rock, classic, or jazz. Audio bloggers also publish their content in `AAC` or `Ogg Vorbis` format, which is the most popular among *nix users. According to Wikipedia, many music bloggers publish content that may violate copyright laws. However, sometimes they manage to avoid it, since most of their contents are either old or not reissued recently and so may not cause monetary damage for the copyright holder. Many audio bloggers also place a notice in their blogs like "*If the owner objects about this post, I will immediately remove it from my blog*". Many commercial music companies also maintain audio blogs and publish their music files as an advertisement to gain popularity.

Video Blogs

Often known as **vlogs**, video blogs are similar to audio blogs except for the type of content they serve. Vlogs distribute video files to Netizens. These blogs became very popular when video streaming was invented and people started getting higher bandwidth connections than they had previously. After the marketing of Apple's iPod or iTune, vlogs became extremely popular. In the iTune community, video blogging is often known as "video podcasting". Some important facts from vlog history include: Yahoo's vlogger community grew to more than 1000 members in June, 2005; Apple declared that its iPod will play video files; and, Apple's iTune store will also serve videos. These days `VlogMap.org` shows vloggers from around the world with the help of Google Earth and Google Maps.

Common Terms

When you enter the world of blogging, you may hear a lot of new terms like posts, comments, trackbacks, and so forth. These are the parts that make a blog successful and usable in the real world. In the following sections, we will discuss in brief what these terms mean.

Post

Posts are the core part of a blog. Every time someone writes an article in a blog, it is known as a post. Whenever a post is made, visitors can make comments and follow-ups. In most of the blog engines, each post has a separate URL, which is also called **permalink**. With the help of different administrative panels, blog users can make posts in their blogs. For example, if a blog is text-based, there must be a system available to write the posts. If it is a photoblog, there must be tools available to manage pictures before posting. In audio blogs, there are also facilities for streaming the audio files.

Comments

Comments are actually follow-ups made to posts by the visitors to a blog. Comments may either be made by anonymous users or may require registration to write. These days many blogs allow anonymous users to comment, but with a necessary spam protection system. Comment spams are those useless automated comments that are simply advertising a product or a website or that are totally irrelevant to a post. These days some online marketing agencies are spreading advertisements via automated bots (bots are "robot" scripts). So if you allow anonymous commenting, be aware of comment spams.

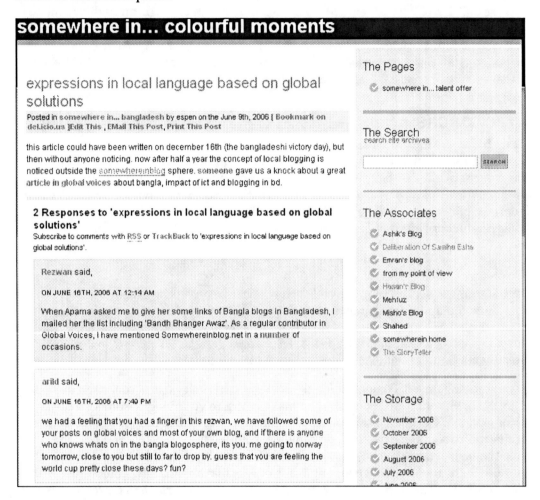

Permalinks

Permalinks are an abbreviation for permanent links. Generally, a permalink is a permanent URL to a specific post in your blog. To optimize blogs for search engines and to make the URLs more readable, people use permalinks. Permalinks are short, straightforward, and easy to remember. In commercial websites with huge content, permanency of URL is a must to provide better marketing and advertising of the content.

Let me show you why permalinks are friendlier with search engines. For example, suppose a URL is in the form `http://example.com/ex.php?id=1&stat=4`. When this page is linked from another site and the robots of search engines get this link, mostly they tend to skip the dynamic part of the URL. That is, the search-engine robots browse only up to `http://example.com/ex.php`, which by no means delivers the exact content you wanted to show. Moreover, consider the permalink URL that refers to the same blog post: `http://blog.example.com/posts/php-lookback-2005`. This is more readable and user-friendly. So permalinks are of great importance to bloggers, if they want to increase their site rank, publicity, and traffic.

Trackbacks

Trackbacks are referral links in which someone refers to your post in their blog. Basically, trackbacks are simple notifications that are sent when someone refers to the content of another blog. When someone trackbacks your post, a link to his or her blog will be displayed as a comment in that article so that you will be aware of all the referrals. However, spammers are also ready to abuse this useful system to advertise their product or websites.

RSS

RSS stands for **Really Simple Syndication**. RSS is a very strong medium to distribute the up-to-date content or news from your website to the people who subscribe to RSS in your blog. WordPress and almost every other blog engine supports auto-generation of RSS feeds. RSS works great as an advertising medium. If you are not familiar with RSS, then let me explain it briefly.

A typical blog post RSS contains a link, a title, and a small excerpt of the ten to fifteen most recent posts. So when you make a post in your blog or someone posts a comment, the RSS updates automatically and your RSS subscriber gets an automatic notification about the update. They can then examine the RSS feeds and find the latest content. These days RSS is a very popular tool, but is highly criticized. This is because there are three independent forms of RSS that are not fully compatible with each other. They are RSS 1.0, RSS 2.0, and RSS 0.91. Atom is rather a more matured syndication system that takes the best from RSS and is developed in a structured way.

Tags

Tags are keywords relevant to your post through which someone may find it. When you make a post, just find some keywords that best describe your post. These keywords are tracked by **Technorati** (see below to know about Technorati) and other indexing tools. For example, if you post about a natural disaster like an earthquake or hurricane, tag it with relevant keywords like land subsidence, earthquake, disaster, and death. When people want to know about recent earthquakes, they may search with one of these terms, which will help your content to come in the front page.

Simply use your common sense for choosing keywords. Don't abuse this tagging feature by using irrelevant tags to increase the traffic. If you abuse, there are chances of being banned from those indexing services and that will cause a major failure in your blogging life.

Please note that some blog engines, for instance Blogger, do not support trackbacks and tags unlike WordPress.

Your Friends in Blogging

Well, what if nobody knows that you have a blog or you blogged recently? Unless you are maintaining a very private blog, there is no value in writing your diaries without a reader. The question is how to let others know about your blogs. Of course, they would not be interested to read that you had a cup of coffee this morning or you slept eight hours last night. To inform people about your worthy content, a search engine is your best friend. So the more frequently you publish your content, the more the search engine robots visit your page. However, there is something really special for bloggers.

Search engine robots or spiders are automated scripts developed by search engine companies that crawl through the websites using the navigation links found on them. These robots just read the content of your page and add it to the search engine database by proper indexing. Thereafter, anyone can reach your page whenever they search for any relevant keyword that was present in your page content.

Technorati is the greatest content-syndication site, which indexes your content with the help of some tags. Technorati has automated trackback URLs, which ping the users when you update your blog. So Technorati indexes your recent update immediately after you make a post on your site and displays your post in that tag category. For example, when someone wants to know what other bloggers are thinking about AJAX, he or she goes to Technorati and searches for the term AJAX. Technorati will display all the blog posts that are indexed by it in different orders like chronologically or as per blog's authority. So you will not only get that information, but also you will be aware of the recent trends. We will learn the details about how to automatically ping Technorati to index your content in Chapter 4. Till then for more information visit Technorati at http://technorati.com.

Another tool that helps you to publish your content for other people is **del.icio. us**. If you read it without the breaks, you will find the word "delicious" in this URL `http://del.icio.us/`. del.icio.us is the largest public bookmark system operated via the same tag mechanism that is found in Technorati except that you have to enter your data manually. So when you make a post, just go to del.icio.us and bookmark your content with some relevant tags so that other people can find your content. If they find your content useful, they will also tag it and day by day it will be more visible to the outer world.

One more tool that you must be aware of is **digg**. This operates with a slightly different mechanism than the previous two. If you update your blog, just go to `http://digg.com/` and submit your news. People can then rate your news by clicking on the **digg** option. The more your content is digged, the more popularity you will get. When people search your content, they get the most digged content on the front page. So you gain a great publicity, if your content is really useful.

All these tools are of very high volume and crawled by search engines every day. So if your URLs are indexed on these sites, no doubt you will get huge publicity. As more people visit your blog, you become more successful in blogging.

Meet the Giants

When you start blogging, you have several options for choosing a blog engine. You can choose a commercial one or a free one; you can choose a tool that suits you perfectly. Before starting a blog, just review the contents of your blog and the audience you are writing for.

In this section, we will see some popular blog engines, review their features, and discuss why WordPress is one of the best among them. We will also see what makes WordPress so perfect and popular, and how WordPress can fit to your needs.

The first name that comes from the history of blogging is Blogger.com (`http://www.blogger.com`). It is one of the earliest blog engines that is still available in the market. It's free to use but not open-sourced at all. You will find a huge blogger community who use Blogger.com.

Next we have the **Blog City**, another old but easy-to-maintain blog engine. You will also find **Yahoo 360** as another great blogging tool these days. Yahoo 360 started in 2005, and came into the spotlight because of its abundance of features. We will also discuss **MSN spaces**, something from Microsoft that is similar to the Yahoo 360 blog. You will also see some of the features of the MovableType and ExpressionEngine blog engines.

We will focus on some of the strong competitors to WordPress like boastMachine, Drupal, Serendipity, b2evolution, and Nucleus. Finally, we will see two other promising alternatives, namely Textpattern and bblog.

Blogger

Blogger is a lightweight blogging engine served by the giant, Google. This is one of the earliest blog engines that made blogging so popular. It is totally free to register an account with Blogger. The key feature of Blogger is its simplicity and its themes. The negative features are its incompatibility with plug-ins, being closed-sourced, and advertisements. Blogger blogs are very friendly with search engines as it is a part of Google- a very popular search engine. You can find Blogger at `http://www.blogger.com`.

Blog City

Administering blogs with Blog City (`www.blog-city.com`), another senior from blogging history, is really simple; it's also free. The feature that will excite you most is its simplicity. Their major goal is hyper minimalism. Although not feature-rich, Blog City is a text-based user-friendly blog engine. The missing features are a photo gallery and eye-splashing themes. Moreover, forced advertisements may be considered as another drawback. Blog City is also slightly heavier to load, i.e. it takes more time to download, than its peers.

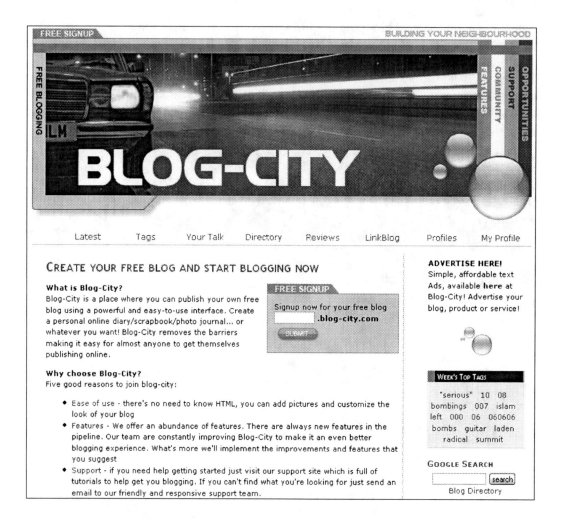

Yahoo 360

Plenty of features make Yahoo 360 one of the coolest blog engines. Yahoo 360 was introduced in 2005. Generally, Yahoo 360 is a social-communicating tool in which blogging is a feature. Integration with a lot of public services like Yahoo photos and Yahoo news makes it efficient and very strong in the market. However, all these things also confuse a blogger whose main target is only blogging. At the time of writing this book, the Yahoo 360 blog didn't support plug-ins.

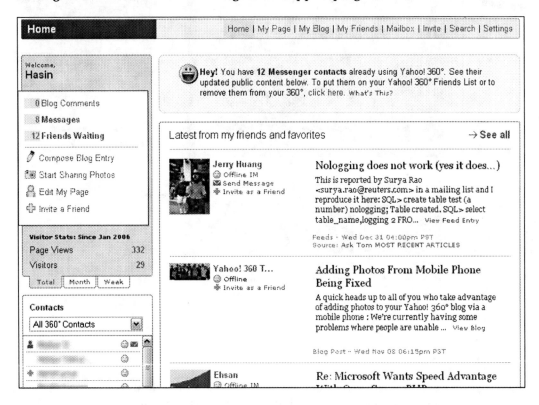

MSN Spaces

MSN spaces (`http://spaces.live.com/`) is the blogging tool introduced by the software giant, Microsoft in December, 2004. This blog is integrated with MSN Messenger and features a photo gallery, capability to SMS content from mobile phones, and integration with MyMSN. There are plenty of features that are not particularly suited for just blogging, but rather for social communication and personalization. MSN spaces serve advertisements in their blogs and the entire blog engine is a little heavyweight.

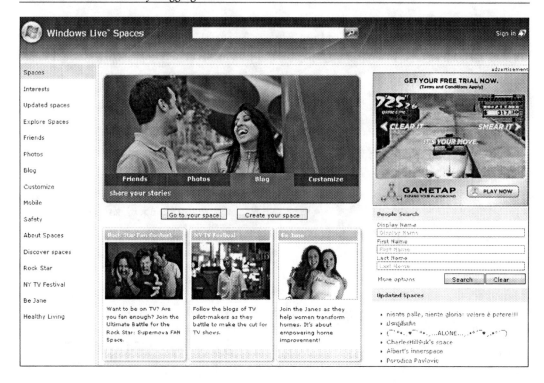

Six Apart

Six Apart (`http://www.sixapart.com/`) is another company that deals with blogging. It developed several popular blogging engines some of which are free while some are not. Among them, MovableType is a very popular blogging engine. MovableType sets the standards for many blogging features and develops one of the three popular blogging APIs (MovableType, MetaWeblog, and Blogger API). The other blogging engines developed by SixApart are Vox (`www.vox.com`), TypePad(`www.typepad.com`), and LiveJournal (`www.livejournal.com/`). Among these, LiveJournal is very popular. You would be surprised if you see some of the statistics of LiveJournal. It is a hosted free blogging engine that has more than 96 million accounts among which 19 million are active. The number of posts per hour is above 18000.

TYPEPAD | MOVABLE TYPE | LIVEJOURNAL | BUSINESS | SUPPORT

Award-winning blogging tools for everyone

Business & Professional Blogging

The choice for professional
and passionate bloggers.
Read More »

MOVABLETYPE
Publishing **Platform**

The first choice for
business.
Read More »

Personal Blogging

The latest in personal
blogging. Coming soon.
Get Invited »

A diverse community of
independent bloggers.
Read More »

FREE! At Six Apart, we believe that personal blogging is priceless. Feel free to start whenever you like.
Try LiveJournal today. Or get on the invitation list for Vox. It's your choice. And it's free...

ExpressionEngine

ExpressionEngine (`http://www.expressionengine.com`) supports a lot of features,
so it is actually more than a blog engine; sometimes it is called a web publishing
engine by its developers. Even when you compare ExpressionEngine with other
CMSs with its features, it will obtain a higher rank. ExpressionEngine is sleek,
powerful, and documented very well by its developers. It has tons of features and
modules. ExpressionEngine is a commercial and costly blogging tool (better say an
advanced CMS), which also supports a very restricted free version with minimal
features. Moreover, its administration panel is quite complicated, which can be
daunting to learn for beginners and non-technical bloggers. ExpressionEngine also
lacks plug-ins, themes, and a huge user community.

ExpressionEngine v 1.4.0				CP Home	User Guide
PUBLISH	**EDIT**	**TEMPLATES**	**COMMUNICATE**	**MODULES**	**MY ACCOUNT**

CP Home > My Account

Member: Admin	Account Statistics For: Admin	
Personal Settings	Email Address	sales@pmachine.com
Subscription Manager	Join Date	2005-06-24 12:19 PM
Private Messages	Last Visit	2006-08-21 09:01 PM
Customize Control Panel	Total Weblog Entries	6
	Total Comments	1
Weblog Settings	Date of Most Recent Entry	2005-06-24 12:31 PM
Extras	Date of Most Recent Comment	2005-06-24 08:39 AM
Member Administration	IP Address:	216.104.73.183
	Most Recent Forum Post	2005-06-24 01:11 PM
	Total Forum Topics	1
	Total Forum Posts	0

Other Blog Engines

Besides these commercial or hosted solutions, there are also some cool free open-source blogging engines. Let us take a look at them.

Serendipity

Serendipity, often called s9y, is a strong competitor to WordPress. It is feature-rich, smooth, and well structured; so no one can skip it at a glance. However, the main problem of s9y is the lack of plug-ins and its heavy weight. s9y takes more bandwidth and time to serve its content than WordPress. However, Serendipity is a neat and very nice blogging tool for those who expect something more than just a blog. In Serendipity, you will have full control over plug-in development and management. This blog engine is compatible with different kinds of database servers like MySQL, PostgreSQL, etc. You will find Serendipity at this URL: www.s9y.org.

boastMachine

Another promising open-source blogging engine that recently came into focus is boastMachine (http://boastology.com/). It features rating of posts, a spam filter, an image manager, etc. By default, all these features are also available with WordPress via plug-ins. boastMachine is a lightweight engine. The main drawback of boastMachine is its incompatibility with plug-ins. Being comparatively new to the blogging market and maintained by a single user, boastMachine lacks a large user community and online help.

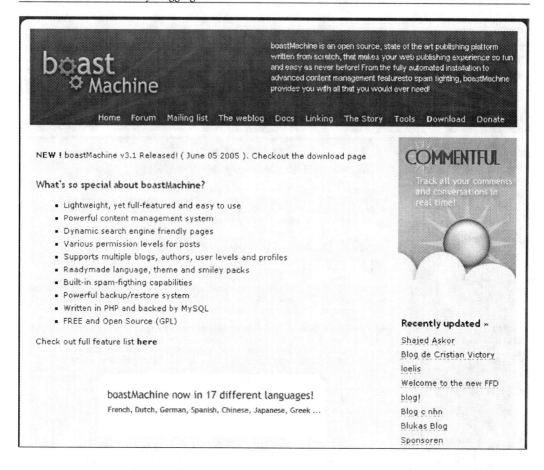

Drupal

Drupal is actually used as a content management system but was originally written by Dries Buytaert as a bulletin-board system. It's a system with very strong architecture featuring plug-ins and themes. Drupal has a huge user community and excellent documentation. Since Drupal's main goal is not blogging, it has plenty of modules that are best suitable for a website. Moreover, Drupal has modules like e-commerce, photo gallery, CVS integration, and mailing list manager. Mailing list manager is a feature through which you can manage a group of users and send mails to them. The Drupal administration panel is quite heavy and confusing for new bloggers. In the real world, there are different modified distributions of Drupal among which CivicSpace is a notable one.

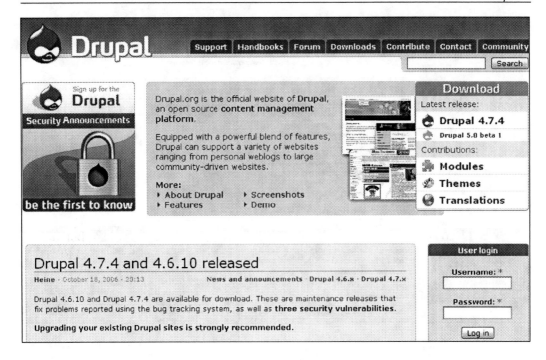

b2evolution

One of the greatest features offered by **b2evolution** (http://b2evolution.net/) is multi-user blogging, which is also present in WordPress via WordPress MU. This means you can host a single blog, but it can be used by multiple users as separate entities. b2evoution features auto-installation with minimum hassle. It's a feature-rich blog engine. One of the greatest drawbacks of b2evolution is the lack of themes and plug-ins. Its administration panel is rich but very confusing. It is comparatively heavier than WordPress.

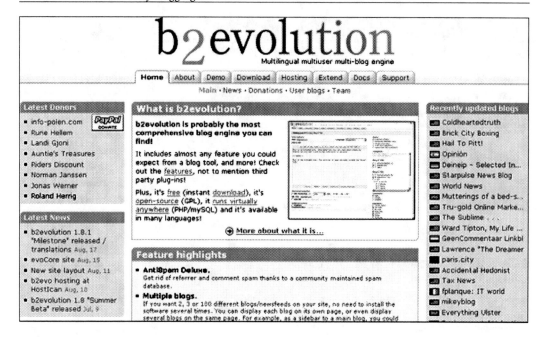

Nucleus CMS

Nucleus CMS (`http://nucleuscms.org/`) is also a popular content management system. It is actually more than a blog engine. Nucleus supports a multi-lingual and multi-author blogging environment. Some other extensive features are the availability of a huge number of templates and plug-ins, an easy administration panel, easy syndication support, etc. Nucleus exposes a rich set of APIs to extend it via plug-ins. Administration of Nucleus is more complicated than that of other blog engines.

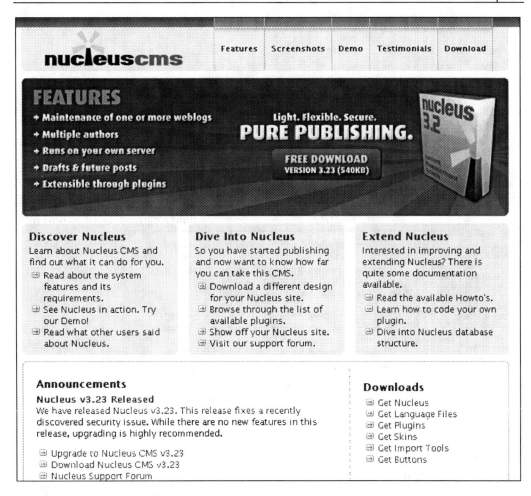

Textpattern

Textpattern (`http://www.textpattern.com/`) is another lightweight blog engine that is compatible with plug-ins. Its main goal is to be a general-purpose CMS system. Textpattern supports multi-lingual blogging via UTF-8. Its feature-richness and easy administration makes it a very strong competitor to WordPress. Textpattern is developed by Dean Allen and is available on the market since early 2001.

TEXTPATTERN

Join the notify list:

you@there

Interface Features
» Quick conversion of plain text to valid XHTML with Textile
» Quickly search old articles by keyword
» Up-to-the-minute visitor/referrer logs
» Browser-based template and CSS editing
» Unlimited site sections
» Unlimited article, link, file and image categories
» Browser-based file and image upload &

What Is It?

A free, flexible, elegant, easy-to-use content management system for all kinds of websites, even weblogs.

When it comes to publishing on the internet, beginners and experts alike are met with a bothersome paradox: word processors and graphics applications allow anyone to do a pretty good job of managing text and images on a personal computer, but to make these available to the worldwide web – a seemingly similar environment of documents and destinations – ease of use vanishes behind sudden requirements for multilingual programming skills, proficiency in computer-based graphic design, and, ultimately, the patience of a saint.

Those who soldier on anyway may find themselves further held back by the web's purported inflexibility with written language, with its reluctance to cope with all but the plainest of text, or by the unpredictable results brought about by using 'WYSIWYG' web editors.

Textpattern is a web application designed to help overcome these and other hurdles to publishing online, and to simplify the

Download
» 4.0.3 (29 Dec 2005) available now

Read
» The weblog
» Some FAQs

Find
» A web host

Places to go
» forum.textpattern.com is open.
» TextBook totally rules.
» So does Textpattern Resources.
» Harvest layouts and more in the Text Garden.
» Hey, there's a magazine!

WordPress

WordPress is comparatively more lightweight than many of its siblings. It is a feature-rich, well-structured blogging engine that has a huge user base. You will find the documentation of WordPress is some of the best documentation ever made. You will also get a very quick response from its user community to any problem you may ever have. There are thousands of contributors who are regularly developing plug-ins and themes. So if any lack of feature is found, you can easily find some good plug-ins to remedy it. Moreover, as a worst-case scenario, if you can't find any plug-in that fulfills your need, you can develop one on your own with the help of the state-of-the-art documentation and plug-in API of WordPress. Installing, administering, and maintaining your blog with WordPress is so easy that you require no previous blogging experience to deliver a world-class blog.

WordPress' admin interface has been redesigned from the ground up to be as intuitive as possible.

Before proceeding further, let us see the complete feature list of WordPress:

- Supports unlimited categories and sub-categories
- Automatic syndication by RSS and Atom
- Uses XML RPC interface for trackbacks and remote posting
- Can cope with email posting
- Supports plug-ins and themes (skinnable)
- Ability to import data from MovableType, Textpattern, Greymatter, b2evolution, and Blogger, which is a great advantage when you want to start your blog from an existing one
- Features extensive documents and a rich set of APIs to extend it
- Very easy to administer and maintain with no blogging experience required
- Very convenient search facility
- Instant publishing of content, no matter how long it is, unlike some other blog engine where it is really a headache to update a simple thing
- Multi-lingual blogging capability

- Very well-structured administration panel with tons of features
- Link manager

With the help of plug-ins and a rich set of APIs, you can modify WordPress to meet your requirements for even a complete website. Finally, WordPress comprises of tons of plug-ins, themes, and a really huge user community that can turn your blogging experience into a happy time.

WordPress is the best tool to start blogging with. Its administration panel will simply help you like a wizard. WordPress recently released version 2.0, which is a great upgrade, and has a lot of eye-catching features. We will cover them in Chapter 4. WordPress is developed in PHP, the world's most highly used scripting language, and uses MySQL as its database back end. So you not only get its cool features, but also the advantage of using the state-of-the-art database and scripting language. No doubt, WordPress will make your blogging life easier than ever. Let us now see some examples of other people's blogs, Codex, and some of its extraordinary themes.

The World of WordPress

WordPress is an open-source blog engine that is developed by Matt Mullenweg and Ryan Boren and released under the GNU General Public License. It's one of the most popular blogging tools among its siblings. WordPress is capable of managing a huge amount of data in a very structured way. Administration of WordPress is very simple, which makes it the first choice for thousands of users.

The name "WordPress" was proposed by one of Matt's friends, Christine Selleck. WordPress gained popularity and major acceptance among millions of users in a very short time. It has a huge user community. As mentioned before, one of the greatest advantages that you find in WordPress is the availability of a lot of plug-ins and themes. The code of WordPress itself is very structured and makes it easier for developers to extend it by plug-ins. Codex, the official helpdesk for WordPress is very rich and it documents almost every piece of functionality delivered by WordPress with a lot of good examples.

We will discuss the pros and cons of using WordPress against its closest competitors later in this book. We will go through almost everything in WordPress. In a nutshell, WordPress is the easiest and the most enjoyable blog engine.

The best place where you can learn the ins and outs of WordPress is its central documentation system, Codex (`http://codex.wordpress.org`). WordPress has a world-class documentation and help system where you can find an answer to almost every question regarding WordPress. Following is a screenshot from Codex:

Codex is divided into several categories and sub-categories for beginners, advanced users, and developers. Just head into the category to which you think your problem belongs. For example, if you find problems regarding installation, kick-starting blogging, or administration just move to the beginners section. If you want to discover more about using plug-ins, syndication, database backup, or moving your blog then head into the advanced category.

If you are interested in extending WordPress by writing plug-ins or decorating your blog with self-developed themes, go straight to the developers section and study the plug-in APIs and theme documentation.

WordPress community also develops a cool forum named bbForum, which is also developed as an open-source forum module. This forum features different categories and sub-categories where you can directly post your problems and get help from thousands of users. You can also post solutions to other people's problems.

The WordPress community is very active and you will find rapid solutions to your problems here.

If you are a WordPress theme or plug-in developer, you can publish your work in the plug-in or theme section of Codex, from where other people can find these updates. WordPress Codex is an interesting place for WordPress geeks.

WordPress comes with a great repository of themes and plug-ins that are contributed by its huge user community. Codex itself is the best place where you can find answers to almost every type of question regarding WordPress.

WordPress also maintains regular gatherings and meet-ups on its IRC channel. If you want to participate just join **#WordPress channel** in `irc.freenode.net` with your favorite IRC client. You will find many developers and can talk to them directly. This is really great fun.

Posting and Participating in WordPress Forum

Whenever you have problems to which you find no answer in Codex, you can go directly to the community forum and post your problem there. While posting just keep in mind that you should tag your post with relevant keywords so that other people who encounter the same type of problem can find it easily.

To post problems in the WordPress community, you have to register a free account. You can visit the URL http://wordpress.org/support/register.php and give your name, email address, and other optional things while registration. If you succeed, you will receive a password delivered to your mailbox. You can log in with that password and username to this community.

WordPress Support » Register

Registration

Profile Information

A password will be mailed to the email address you provide. Make sure to whitelist our domain (http://wordpress.org) so the confirmation email doesn't get caught by any filters.

Username*:

Email*:

Website:

Location:

Occupation:

Interests:

*These items are required.

Mailing Lists

☑ Subscribe to announcement list (a few messages a year)

Register »

If you go to the WordPress support forums at http://wordpress.org/support, then you will find the following categories. Just select a category for your problem and post in that category. If you post in the wrong category, there are severe chances that you won't get a proper reply.

FORUMS

MAIN THEME	TOPICS	POSTS
Installation — Problems with getting it running.	5,681	30,615
How-To and Troubleshooting — Once it's running	26,369	129,538
Themes and Templates — XHTML and CSS	6,503	37,096
Plugins and Hacks — Extensions and modifications	7,481	43,837
Requests and Feedback — Feature requests; criticism.	2,308	11,036
Your WordPress — Strut your stuff.	2,625	15,185
Miscellaneous — Almost everything else.	2,762	15,422
2.0 Beta — For discussing the 2.0 Beta	329	1,941

Finding Themes for WordPress

There are thousands of theme developers for WordPress and most of their work free for public use. They all use some specific repository to publish their themes. The best source of themes and plug-ins is Codex. Let us look at the following URLs for themes:

- Codex at `http://codex.wordpress.org/Using_Themes/Theme_List`

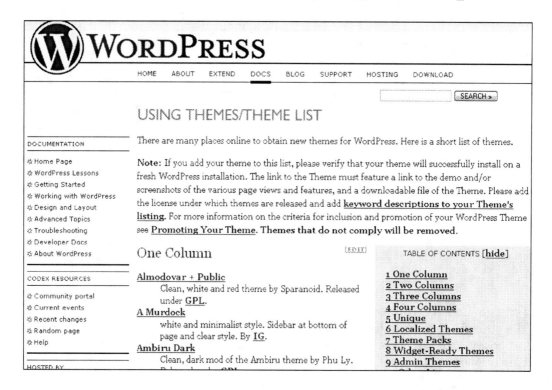

- Alex King's theme repository at `http://alexking.org`

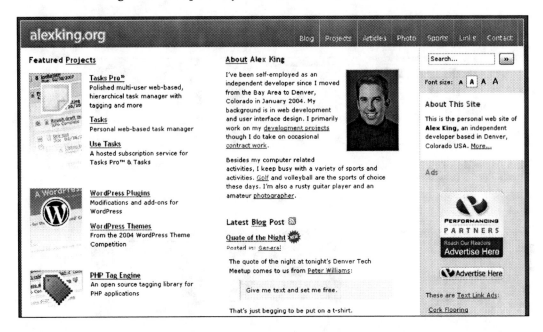

- Blogging Pro theme list at `http://www.bloggingpro.com`

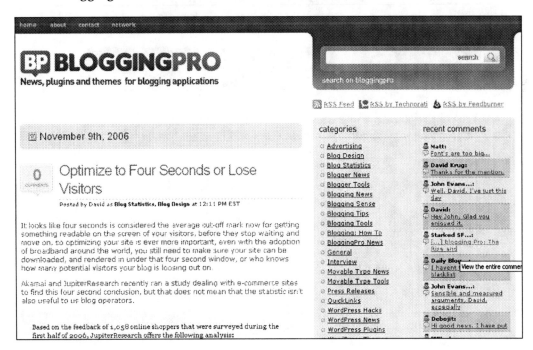

- Themes at `http://www.themes.wordpress.net`

- You will also find some themes developed by me at
  `http://hasin.wordpress.com/my-wordpress-themes/`

If you want to develop themes, then the following URL is the best tutorial you can have:

- UrbanGiraffe at:
  http://www.urbangiraffe.com/2005/04/12/themeguide1/1/

To be informed about the arrival of new themes always visit the themes section in Codex and see the themes marked as new.

Finding Plug-Ins and WordPress News

Plug-ins are the most exciting feature of WordPress. They are small pieces of code that can be managed from the administration panel. The WordPress plug-in management system is so flexible that if you upload your plug-ins in the plug-in folder, you will immediately get access to them via the plug-in section of the administration panel. You can also activate and de-activate them instantly.

WordPress plug-ins are basically meant to extend WordPress features. For example, if you want to add a photo gallery and a photo management system in conjunction with the world's best photo-sharing system Flickr (http://www.flickr.com), you can use FAlbum. You can syndicate RSS in your post using RSS processor plug-ins, which we will develop later in Chapter 9. You can do almost everything you want to do by using these plug-ins.

The best sources of plug-ins available over the net are the following:

- The plug-ins at http://wp-plugins.net

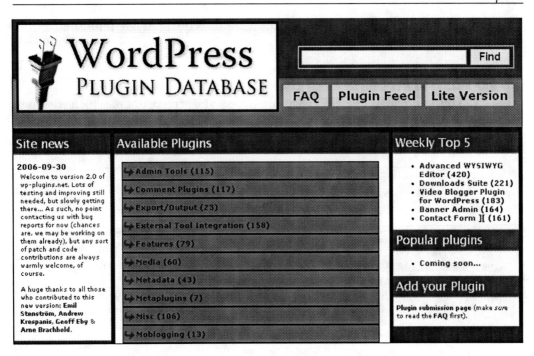

- The plug-ins at `http://codex.wordpress.org/Plugins`

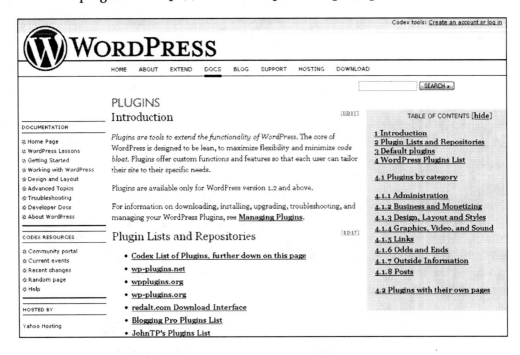

There are several sites where news and events about WordPress are published daily or as soon as they are available. Moreover, there are several sites where you can find news about themes and plug-ins. The following are three up-to-date news sources of WordPress.

- Blogging Pro at `http://bloggingpro.com`, the screenshot of which we have seen earlier in this chapter

- WordPress Station at `http://wpstation.com`

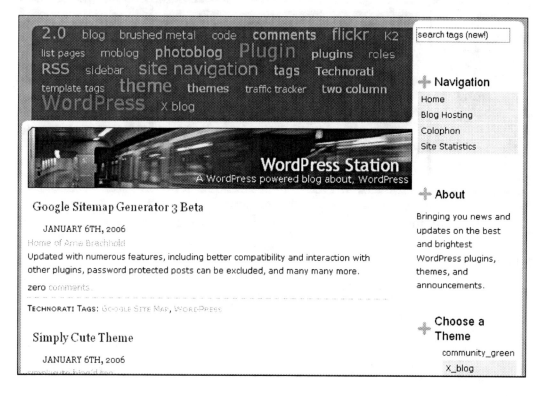

- And of course, Codex

Moreover, if you want to keep yourself up to date about new or upgraded releases of WordPress, you can sign in to its mailing list from the download page. When you subscribe, you will receive all upcoming news directly into your mailbox as the WordPress newsletter. Just notice that there is a mailing list subscribing system available at the bottom of the page (`http://wordpress.org/download/`). This feature really comes handy to keep yourself notified.

Summary

In this chapter, you have been made familiar with blogging and different types of blogging software. You have also seen the major benefits of using WordPress over other blog engines. WordPress is solely devoted to blogging, but you can also use it as a complete CMS with minimal hassle. Moreover, you will gain a lot of popularity with the WordPress community, if you develop themes and plug-ins. In the next chapter, we will discuss how to grab WordPress, set it up, and kick-start blogging.

2
Getting Started with WordPress

In the last chapter, you learned about blogging, its types, and the necessary blogging terms. This chapter will guide you through the process of setting up WordPress and customizing the basic features. WordPress is very small in size, easy to install, and easy to administer. This chapter will show you the different processes for installing WordPress and for setting it up.

WordPress is available in easily-downloadable formats from its website at `http://wordpress.org/download/`. Currently, WordPress version 2.0.5 is available for download. WordPress is a free open-source application, which means you need not pay a single penny for whatever purpose you use it. WordPress is released under the GNU General Public License (GPL). If you are not familiar with the popularity statistics of WordPress, here is an exciting piece of news for you. The previous stable version of WordPress (version 1.5) had been downloaded more than 900,000 times. The recent version 2.0 has already been downloaded more than 1,316,092 times till the time of writing this book.

There is also a different version of WordPress with a multi-user blogging flavor, i.e. several users can maintain their blog separately with a single installation of WordPress. They can register and maintain their blogs independently of one another. This special version of WordPress is neither stable nor mature enough. Moreover, it is not officially supported. This version of WordPress is known as **WordPress MU** or WordPress multi user. In this chapter, we will only cover the installation of WordPress; however, we will discuss WordPress MU in Chapter 10.

Registering a Free Blog at WordPress.com

WordPress.com (`http://www.wordpress.com`) is a hosted service of the WordPress developers where you can register your blog for free. As it is a hosted service, you may not get complete freedom for doing all the things that are possible in a blog hosted by yourself. Especially, in WordPress.com you cannot upload your own theme or edit it unless you pay for it. However, even without that specific feature, WordPress.com is a great place to maintain your personal blog. I also have maintained my personal blog at WordPress.com for a long time. You can find my blog at `http://hasin.wordpress.com`.

To register your free blog, click on the **Get a WordPress Blog Now** link at the top-right corner. You will be redirected to the following page:

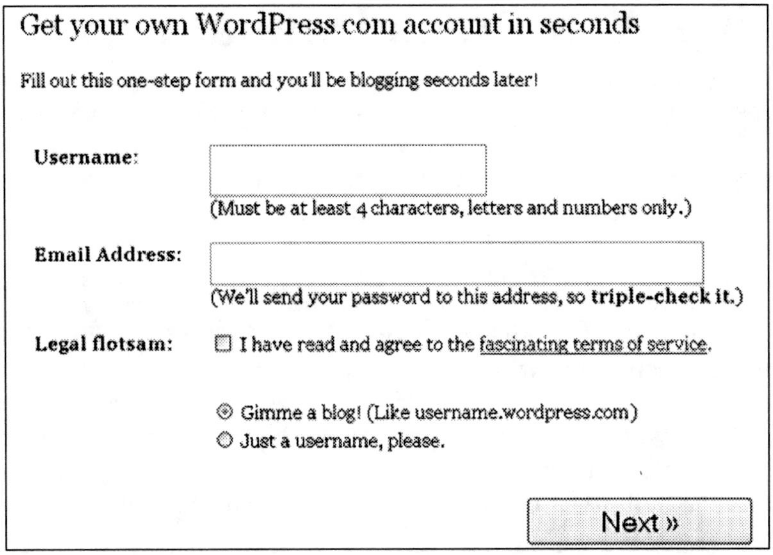

Get your own WordPress.com account in seconds

Fill out this one-step form and you'll be blogging seconds later!

Username: [   ]
(Must be at least 4 characters, letters and numbers only.)

Email Address: [   ]
(We'll send your password to this address, so **triple-check it**.)

Legal flotsam: ☐ I have read and agree to the <u>fascinating terms of service</u>.

⦿ Gimme a blog! (Like username.wordpress.com)
○ Just a username, please.

[Next »]

Type your desired username and email address. Please be sure to check the license agreement checkbox as well as the **Gimme a blog!** checkbox.

After providing this information and clicking on the **Next** button, WordPress will ask for your **Blog Domain, Blog Title,** and **Language** as shown in following screenshot. You can also check if it's a private blog or not. Please notice that you cannot change the blog domain later. So be sure before submitting.

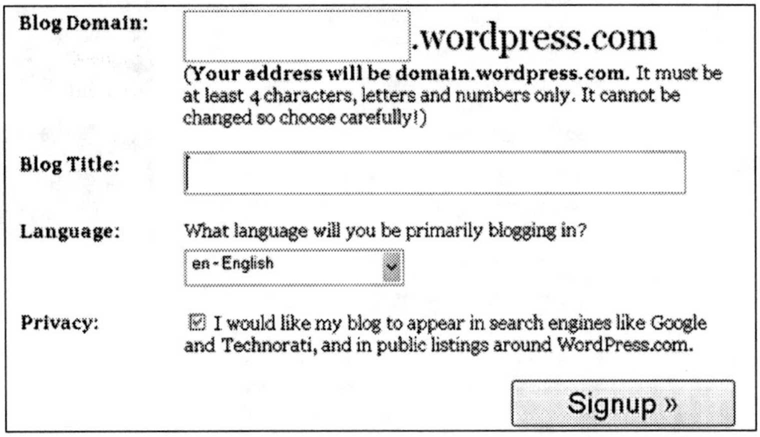

Blog Domain: [   ]**.wordpress.com**
(**Your address will be domain.wordpress.com**. It must be at least 4 characters, letters and numbers only. It cannot be changed so choose carefully!)

Blog Title: [   ]

Language: What language will you be primarily blogging in?
[en - English ▼]

Privacy: ☑ I would like my blog to appear in search engines like Google and Technorati, and in public listings around WordPress.com.

[Signup »]

After providing this information and clicking on **Signup**, you will successfully register your blog in WordPress.com. However, remember that WordPress.com will send you an email with an activation link in it. You must click on it in order to activate your blog.

Installing WordPress Manually

As I said before, WordPress can be downloaded for a manual installation, which is extremely easy and requires no previous programming skills or advanced blog-user experience. It's simply some kind of ready-set-go type of blogging engine where you can easily start even if you are blogging for the first time. For the automatic installation, we will discuss how to set it up with the different administration tools available in cPanel.

First of all, download WordPress from its website at `http://wordpress.org/ download/`. It is available in both Gzip (`tar.gz`) and ZIP (`.zip`) format. Take a look at the following screenshot in which the download links are available on the right side; you may download either of them. If you are using Windows XP or Linux operating systems, you don't need to have any unzipping utility for extracting. Windows XP and later versions can directly extract files from compressed ZIP files. You will also get a built-in extraction facility if you are using Linux.

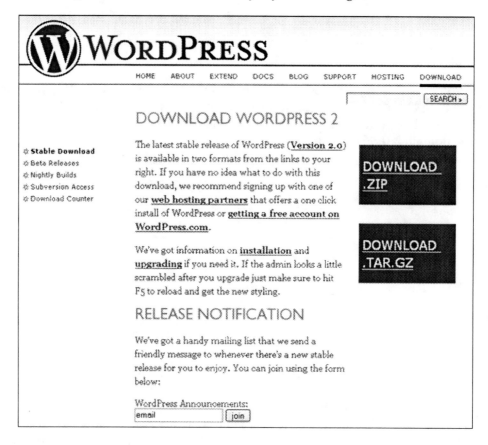

Before installing WordPress, please check the minimal requirements. You must have a web server that supports PHP. The best web server that you can count on is Apache. For PHP, you must have at least version 4.2 or later installed on your machine. WordPress will also run with PHP 5.x.x series without any problem. Besides, you require a MySQL database server; you must have at least MySQL version 3.23.23 or later installed on your machine. You may also have a local or remote MySQL server with complete privileges to create tables required for WordPress. If your web server meets all these requirements, it is surely ready to proceed further. Let us take a look at these minimum requirements once again. Apache `mod_rewrite` is also required for a user-friendly URL.

Apache `mod_rewrite` is installed by default in most web hosting accounts. If you are hosting your own account, you can enable `mod_rewrite` by modifying the Apache web server configuration file. You can check the URL `http://www.tutorio.com/tutorial/enable-mod-rewrite-on-apache` to know how to enable `mod_rewrite` on your web server. If you are running on shared hosting, then ask your system administrator to install it for you. However, it is more likely that you already have it installed on your hosting account.

Let us download the archive (either in `.zip` or `.tar.gz` format) of WordPress. Besides the remote installation of WordPress, I strongly suggest installing a local version as well. If you plan to develop themes or plug-ins, testing and deploying them directly to the remote server may require more time than testing and deploying them locally. Let us try the remote installation. If you extract the WordPress ZIP file, it will look something like this:

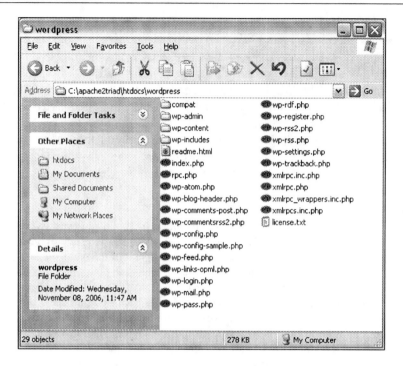

 Just note that there is a `readme.html` file inside this folder that gives you a very good introduction to many different features of WordPress.

Now we need to upload all these files to our website using any FTP client. There are several FTP clients available on the Internet for free usage (or as a shareware). Here we will use Filezilla (`http://filezilla.sourceforge.net/`) as an FTP client to connect to our FTP server and then upload these files. Following is a step-by-step guide to the installation process.

 You can also use the popular web-based FTP applications Net2FTP at `http://www.net2ftp.com` or Web2FTP at `http://web2ftp.com`. Using these packages, you can upload archives from the Internet and they will automatically uncompress the archive. I found it really useful, because now I can always stay in touch with my FTP server without installing any desktop application.

Step 1: Connect to your FTP Server

Using any FTP client, just connect to your FTP server and open the folder where you want to upload these files. I am using Filezilla as an FTP client here. After connecting to your FTP server, you will see the following window. (I am uploading my file in `phpxperts.com` in the **testwp** folder.)

On the left side, you will see the files from your local folder, and on the right side, you will see your remote folder.

Step 2: Upload the Files

Just locate the extracted WordPress files on your local machine from the left pane and drag all of them onto the right pane. You will see that all these files have been queued to be uploaded.

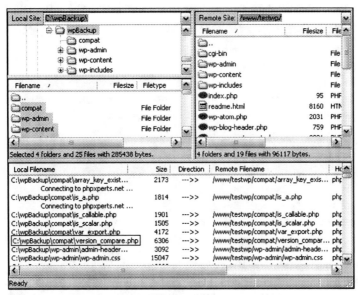

File transfer will then start automatically.

Step 3: Install

Now it's time to install WordPress. For example, I just uploaded all my files at the URL http://www.phpxperts.net/WordPress. So this is going to be the URL of my WordPress blog. If you access your WordPress URL via your browser, it will look like this:

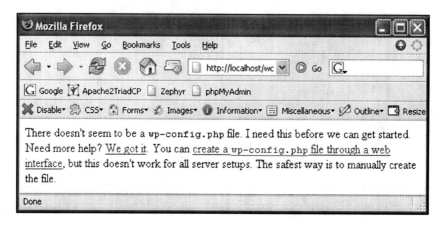

It says that you need to configure a file named wp-config.php before proceeding further. Open the WordPress folder and find the file named wp-config-sample.php. You have to rename this file as wp-config.php and modify its content. However, keep a backup of the original wp-config-sample.php file somewhere else for in case of problems. Don't worry; you need not be a PHP programmer for editing this file. Just open this file with a simple editor like VI or Notepad. The following is an example of the original wp-config.php file:

```php
<?php
// ** MySQL settings ** //
define('DB_NAME', 'WordPress');    // The name of the database
define('DB_USER', 'username');     // Your MySQL username
define('DB_PASSWORD', 'password'); // and password
define('DB_HOST', 'localhost');    // 99% chance you won't need to
change this value

// You can have multiple installations in one database if you give
each a unique prefix
$table_prefix = 'wp_';
// Only numbers, letters, and underscores please!

// Change this to localize WordPress.  A corresponding MO file for the
chosen language must be installed to wp-includes/languages.
// For example, install demo to wp-includes/languages and set WPLANG
to 'de' to enable German language support.
```

```
define ('WPLANG', '');

/* That's all, stop editing! Happy blogging. */

define('ABSPATH', dirname(__FILE__).'/');
require_once(ABSPATH.'wp-settings.php');
?>
```

There are several parameters for setting up a successful connection to the MySQL database. You now have to modify them so that they match the original settings of your MySQL database. If you already have a web hosting account, then you probably know the MySQL database details (i.e. database name, username, and password) for your account. If you don't have this data, please contact your web host providers for it. If you have cPanel in your web hosting account, you may create databases from the MySQL administration panel (depending on how many databases you can create for your hosting account). We will now discuss how to create a database from cPanel.

 Well, it's not mandatory that you need cPanel in your hosting account to create databases. Sometimes it is also possible to create databases using Ensim, HSphere, or Plesk. If you have shell or secured shell access, you can achieve this functionality by giving commands.

To create a database from cPanel, log into cPanel and click on the "MySQL database" icon. You will get a page showing the details of your database entries. In this page, you will see a portion where you can create new databases as shown in the following screenshot:

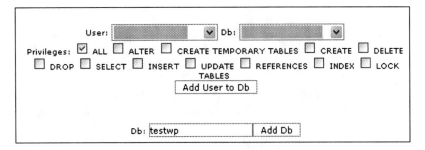

Just enter the name of your database and click on the **Add Db** button; it will be created instantly. If database creation is successful, you will get the following confirmation:

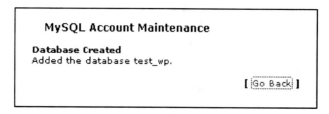

If you click on the **Go Back** link, you will reach the previous page where your database is listed in the available **Db** drop-down box. Now the next task is to create a user and assign that user to your database.

Enter a username and password into the text field and click on the **Add User** button. You will get a confirmation after successfully creating a user.

Let us assign full privilege to this newly created user of the database that you just created. Select the newly created user from the **User** drop-down list and the database from the **Db** list. Please ensure that you have marked the checkbox for **All**. Finally, click on the **Add User to Db** button, and that's it!

You can use this data for a custom WordPress installation.

If you are testing a WordPress installation on your local PHP, Apache, and MySQL installation, please log into your MySQL client and execute the following command to create a database:

```
mysql> create database wp;
```

After creating the database, modify the `wp-config.php` file with the proper parameters. Actually, all we change here are the database parameters. For my machine, the `wp-config.php` file after modification looks like this:

```php
<?php
// ** MySQL settings ** //
define('DB_NAME', 'wp');        // The name of the database
define('DB_USER', 'hasin');        // Your MySQL username
define('DB_PASSWORD', 'WordPress!@#$%'); // ...and password
define('DB_HOST', 'localhost');     // 99% chance you won't need to
change this value

// You can have multiple installations in one database if you give
each a unique prefix

$table_prefix  = 'wp_';    // Only numbers, letters, and underscores
please!

// Change this to localize WordPress.  A corresponding MO file for the
chosen language must be installed to wp-includes/languages.
// For example, install demo to wp-includes/languages and set WPLANG
to 'de' to enable German language support.

define ('WPLANG', '');

/* That's all, stop editing! Happy blogging. */

define('ABSPATH', dirname(__FILE__).'/');
require_once(ABSPATH.'wp-settings.php');
?>
```

If you have only one MySQL database in your web-hosting account and you don't have permission to create more, then the $table_prefix setting in wp-config.php is extremely helpful. For WordPress installation, this setting is used as a prefix for each table name; so there are no conflicts in between the existing tables and the newly created tables. By changing this setting, you can install as many WordPress installations as you want using a single MySQL database.

Note that I did not make any changes after the fifth line. Now again locate the WordPress URL via your browser. It now looks something like the following screenshot. Here, you will get a link to **install.php**.

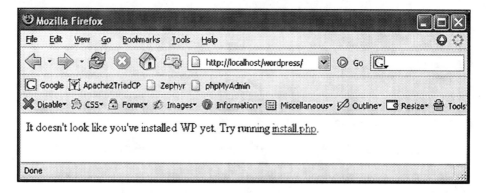

Click on this **install.php** hyperlink. It will redirect you to the following installation page:

Proceed further by clicking on **First Step**. This will redirect you to a page where you have to insert some basic settings about your blog.

Fill out the **Weblog title** and **Your e-mail** fields properly. The weblog title will be the title of your blog, and for all communication purposes WordPress will use this email address to communicate with you. So you must provide a valid email address. Now it's time to click and go to the second step. Do it and you will see something like the following screenshot:

If you reach the page above, you have installed WordPress successfully in your hosting account. Just note that this page gives you an auto-generated password for your admin account. For my installation, it is **3564ff** as you can see in the screenshot. This page also contains the link to the admin panel of your WordPress installation as **wp-login.php**. For later use, just note that you can get access to the admin panel via the URL `http://your_WordPress_installation_path/wp-login.php`.

Installing WordPress from the cPanel

We will now learn how to install WordPress automatically via Fantastico in cPanel and then log into the WordPress admin panel. There is no guarantee that you have Fantastico in your cPanel because it is a value-added service. Just log into your cPanel, and search for the word Fantastico. If you have it, you will find it. Follow these steps to get WordPress automatically installed on your hosting account.

Firstly, click on **Fantastico**. The following screenshot is a typical view of Fantastico after you get in. Note that you will find **WordPress** in the **Blogs** section of Fantastico. To start the automated installation, click on **WordPress**.

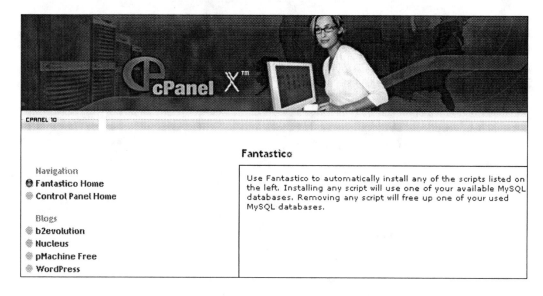

Next, click on **New Installation**.

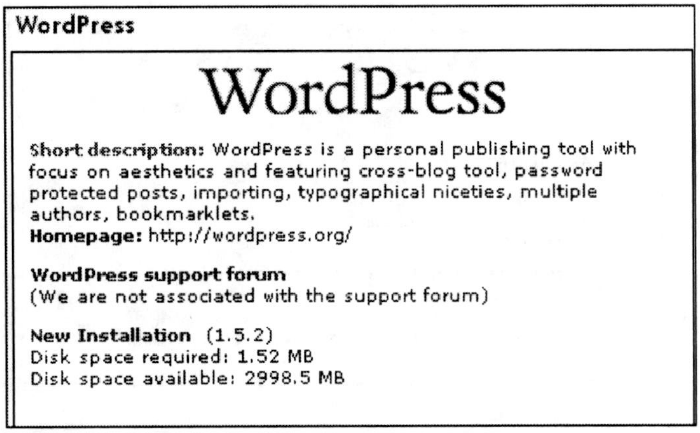

```
WordPress

              WordPress

Short description: WordPress is a personal publishing tool with
focus on aesthetics and featuring cross-blog tool, password
protected posts, importing, typographical niceties, multiple
authors, bookmarklets.
Homepage: http://wordpress.org/

WordPress support forum
(We are not associated with the support forum)

New Installation  (1.5.2)
Disk space required: 1.52 MB
Disk space available: 2998.5 MB
```

The screenshot opposite shows the page filled with sample data. If you want to enable blogging by email, then you have to fill out the email parameters with valid data. Please note that the data you give here as **Site name** will be the title of your blog. After entering the necessary data, click on **Install WordPress**.

WordPress

WordPress

Install WordPress (1/3)

Installation location

Install on domain phpxperts.com

Install in directory testwp

Leave empty to install in the root directory of the domain (access example: http://domain/).
Enter only the directory name to install in a directory (for **http://domain/name/** enter **name** only). This directory SHOULD NOT exist, it will be automatically created!

Admin access data

Administrator-username (you need this to enter the protected admin area) test-admin

Password (you need this to enter the protected admin area) -password

Base configuration

Admin nickname tester

Admin e-mail (your email address) myemail

Site name my site title

Description

E-mail account configuration

E-mail account username test

E-mail account password test

POP/SMTP server test

POP/SMTP server port 110

Install WordPress

This is the final screen. Just click on **Finish Installation** to be redirected to the next page.

In the following page, you have to enter a valid email address. The details of your WordPress installation will be mailed to that address.

That's all for installing WordPress from cPanel.

Upgrading WordPress from Older Installations

If you have an older version of WordPress installed and want to upgrade it instead of making an entirely new installation, the following steps will guide you through:

As a first step, you must do the following for the security of your databases and files:

1. You must back up your WordPress database. If anything goes wrong while upgrading (there is a greater chance that everything will go fine), you may lose your database content.

2. You must back up all your WordPress files in the WordPress directory, even including the `.htaccess` file, if present.

3. Verify that these backups are not corrupted and you can use them later when required. If your Internet connection breaks during the download, you may have a corrupted file. So always try to check the backups to see whether you can unzip them.

4. Deactivate all your plug-ins. Deactivating plug-ins is a must, since some plug-ins may not work with the new coding structure of WordPress and these plug-ins may cause instability to your new WordPress installation. So before proceeding further, please ensure that you have already disabled all your plug-ins from your WordPress admin panel plug-ins section.

 Warning: Do not start the upgrade process unless you have ensured that the preceding four steps are completed.

To upgrade completely, the following steps have to be performed:

5. Delete your old WordPress files except the following:
    ○ `wp-config.php` file
    ○ `wp-content` folder
    ○ `wp-images` folder
    ○ `wp-includes/languages` folder
    ○ `.htaccess` file, if you used custom `mod_rewrite` rules for your previous WordPress site

6. Upload the new WordPress files to your previous WordPress folder. Some of the files may be automatically re-written. For now, just allow overwriting your files.

7. Run the WordPress upgrade and follow the necessary instructions from that page. You can access the upgrade page from this URL: `http://example.com/wp-admin/upgrade.php`.

8. Upgrade your permalink setup to what it was before. If you wrote it in the `.htaccess` file, upgrade the `.htaccess` file according to the previous one. You have not yet been introduced to managing permalinks; that will come in the later chapters. You will then understand the importance of this step.

9. Upgrade your plug-ins and themes. The new WordPress installation may break backward compatibility for some plug-ins. So plug-in developers may release new versions of their plug-ins that are compatible with this new version of WordPress. Just check the plug-ins that work with this version of WordPress from `http://codex.WordPress.org/User:Matt/ 2.0_Plugin_Compatibility`.

10. Log in to the admin panel and activate your necessary plug-ins.

11. Finally, just ensure that all the features are working well.

We hope that you now have an upgraded version of WordPress running in your machine.

Basic Troubleshooting during Installation

After the completion of the WordPress installation, you may come across some basic problems. If there were some problems during installation, you may not have a proper output. We will discuss some of these problems and help you to get rid of them in Chapter 10. For now, you can visit the Codex site at `http://codex.WordPress.org` for some basic troubleshooting FAQ.

Logging into the Admin Panel

After a successful installation, it's time to get started. Let us log into the admin panel of WordPress to make some basic configurations. You must do it to get your blog up and running properly.

You can always log into the WordPress admin panel via the URL `http://your_WordPress_installation_path/wp-login.php` (for example, `www.phpxperts.com/testwp/wp-login.php`). You will see the following page:

On this page, you also get an option to retrieve your lost password. For now, just enter your username that is by default "admin" and the password that you got during installation.

The WordPress admin panel displays tons of interesting features in a very structured way. We will get familiar with them with the passage of time. For now, we will only stick with those features that are necessary after a successful installation. Following is a screenshot of the WordPress admin panel that I see just after logging into my personal blog:

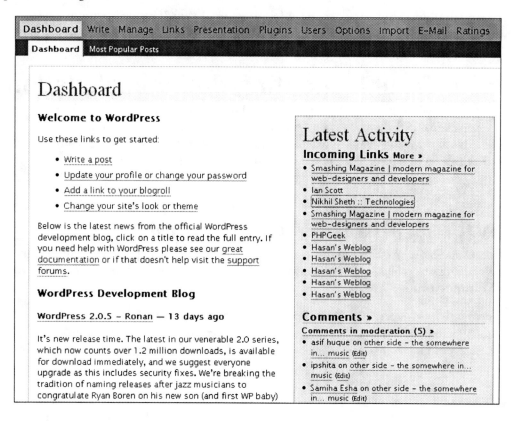

By default, the screen that you see just after login is called **Dashboard**. Here, you get some necessary and important information. From the dashboard, you can start basic things, start comment moderation, and see your recent posts and comments. The dashboard is a very important feature of WordPress.

Just below your blog title, notice a menu bar with different options like **Dashboard**, **Write**, **Manage**, and so forth.

If you remember, during the final stage of manual installation (not from cPanel), you got a password with the help of which you logged into the admin panel just now. To keep such a password in mind would be a difficult task for many. So the first thing we are going to do is change that password into something more easy and readable.

Changing the Password

You can change your login information and password from the **Users** menu. Clicking on it, you will get a page where you can change your credentials and basic information. To change the password, locate the rectangle outlined in the following screenshot:

You can change a lot of information from here. Enter your desired new password and update by clicking the **Update Profile** button at the bottom-right corner. If you are successful, you will get a notice saying **Profile Updated**.

You need to change another important feature in this page. This is how other people see you in your blog. You can change this setting from the drop-down box named **Display name publicly as**. Select admin or your name from it. Just don't let others see you as your email address, which is the default. This may cause you to get a lot of spam in your mail box.

Changing General Blog Information

You may need to change some general blog information like blog title, blog slogan, and so forth after a successful installation to kick-start blogging. For this, you can head towards **General Options** by clicking on the **Options** menu.

There are many options to play with, but we will only look at those options that are necessary as basic blog information. Here, you can enter your **Weblog title**, blog slogan as **Tagline, E-mail address, Membership, New User Default Role**, and **Date and Time** data. Most of these options are familiar to you except membership and new user role. WordPress is a blog engine where many users can blog at a single place if you allow them to write, after being registered. This means that they don't get a separate blog for themselves, but rather a single place where they can all contribute. They may have roles and privileges, and they can do a lot of things according to their roles. So be careful about these two settings.

General Options

Weblog title:	My First Blog
Tagline:	Just another WordPress weblog
	In a few words, explain what this weblog is about.
WordPress address (URI):	http://localhost/wordpress
Blog address (URI):	http://localhost/wordpress
	If you want your blog homepage to be different than the directory you installed WordPress in, enter that address here.
E-mail address:	myemail@mydomain.org
	This address is used only for admin purposes.
Membership:	☐ Anyone can register ☐ Users must be registered and logged in to comment
New User Default Role:	Subscriber ▾

There are two options available under **Membership**: one is **Anyone Can Register** and another one is **Users must be registered and logged in to comment**. The first one indicates that anyone can register in your blog and start having some fun. They can register themselves into your blog via the URL `http://your_WordPress_installation_path/wp-register.php`. If you turn the first option on, you will see something like the following when you visit that URL:

If you don't allow public registration, you will get the following page:

If you don't need multiple users in your blog, it is suggested to turn this feature off because of possible security breaches. Moreover, this feature is not needed when you are maintaining your blog by yourself.

There is another setting that works in conjunction with the previous setting. This is the **New User Default Role** option, which means what should be the role when a user registers in your blog. If you allow public registration, just keep the setting as is, i.e. **subscriber**. Users as subscribers have minimal control over your blog unless you promote them to "Administrator", "Editor", "Author", or "Contributor". So by making them a subscriber when they register in your blog for the first time, you have less possibility of security breaches. Please ensure that you don't set them as an administrator, by default, else it might prove disastrous.

You can also change the date and time settings from the **General Options** page. Here **UTC time** means "Universal Time Coordinated". This is same as GMT or Greenwich Mean Time. You can set it appropriately according to your time zone. For example, I live in Bangladesh and it's a +6 GMT timezone. So I would set the time in the **Times in the weblog should differ by** field to **6**. If you are living in Canada, your timezone is GMT **-6**. So you will use **-6** for this setting.

Posting your First Post

We have made a lot of settings and gone through several options. Now it's time to starting blogging. The core of any blog is a post, so you are going to make your first post. To post content, you can start by going to the dashboard and clicking on **Write a post** or you may directly click on **Write** from the menu bar. Here is what you see after you get in.

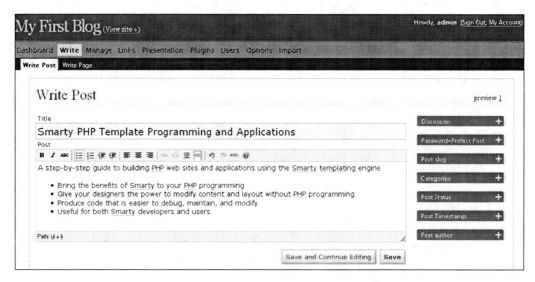

Every post should have a title and some content. There are many other options on this page, but we will discuss them in more detail in Chapter 4. For now, we will just write a sample article and post it. Write the title as you want and click on the **Publish** button once you are done. Don't worry about the sample post. You can manage your posts, edit them, or delete them anytime you want. So for now just make a post to start.

After posting, you can view your blog by clicking on **View site** in the top bar of the admin panel, just right after your blog title. You should see something like this:

The WordPress post page features a rich WYSIWYG (What You See Is What You Get) editor through which you can post contents in your blog. We will discuss it later in detail in Chapter 4.

Making a Comment

When you read your blog, you may see many outsiders making comments on your posts. You may also need to post comment on some of your posts in other blogs. Here we will discuss how we can make a comment on a specific post. We will comment on the post we just made.

You will notice a link saying **No Comments** just below your post. You can post comments by clicking on it, which will take you to the following page:

Smarty PHP Template Programming and Applications

A step-by-step guide to building PHP web sites and applications using the Smarty templating engine

- Bring the benefits of Smarty to your PHP programming
- Give your designers the power to modify content and layout without PHP programming
- Produce code that is easier to debug, maintain, and modify
- Useful for both Smarty developers and users

This entry was posted on Wednesday, September 6th, 2006 at 6:09 am and is filed under Uncategorized. You can follow any responses to this entry through the RSS 2.0 feed. You can leave a response, or trackback from your own site. Edit this entry.

Leave a Reply

Logged in as admin. Logout »

```
                                                    Submit Comment
```

Write anything here and submit your comment. If you make a successful comment, you will see something like this just under the content of your post.

admin Says:
January 15th, 2006 at 10:39 pm e

Wow, Hagen and Packt are doing real great stuff

Retrieving a Lost Password

If you have lost your password and can't get into your admin panel, you can easily retrieve your password by clicking on the **lost your password?** button on the login page. A newly generated password will be instantly mailed to you at the email address given by you during or after installing WordPress via the **General Options** page. So always enter a valid email address; otherwise, it will be a big problem to retrieve lost passwords.

Summary

You have learned a lot of things from this chapter. Now you are able to install WordPress, make posts and comment on those posts totally by yourself. You have also learned how to change different administrative options for your blog. In the next chapter, we will discuss in detail the features for choosing and installing themes. In the meantime, play with these fun-filled features that you just learned about in this chapter.

3
Choosing and Installing Themes

In content management systems, it is a necessary feature to be able to change the look and feel of your website without knowing how to code in HTML and CSS. Almost every CMS supports the facility to allow users to change the look of their site. These managed looks are usually called **themes**. There are thousands of themes available for download free of cost. These themes are developed by members of the WordPress community and listed in a separate section in codex (`http://Codex.wordpress.org/themes`). Before using any theme, you should know some of the basic things about them. You must know how to install them, how to choose the themes that best suit your content and audience, and how to modify static content inside these themes. In this chapter, we will discuss all of these.

This chapter is a ground-up guide to using themes. The advanced topic of developing themes of your own will be discussed in a later chapter.

Finding Themes

Themes are basically distributed as compressed archives. To use them, all you have to do is to unzip them and place them in a special folder inside your WordPress directory, so it is not a complex process to do on your own. There are different websites where you can find themes in a downloadable format. Most of the theme developers offer their themes for free; however, a very few of them offer their themes for a few bucks. Some also offer customized themes according to your need, but of course that is considered as a paid service. If you are not satisfied with what you get for free, you may go for specialized themes. However, it is not a wise decision to head towards paid themes if you can get a similar one for free. If you finish this book step by step, you will also be able to develop themes totally by yourself.

Let us find some themes for our use. These themes are listed in mainly two categories, two-column themes and three-column themes. However, there are also one-column themes and four-column themes available in the community. Some of these themes are minimal and text-based; some of them are graphical. We will also see some of the very common themes well reputed by the WordPress community.

The Official WordPress Theme Page

WordPress distributes some beautiful themes from its original site. These are six in number, and are easy to experiment with. The URL for downloading these themes is http://wordpress.org/extend/themes/. You will find the Green Marine, Blix, Connections, Ocadia, Pool, and Almost Spring themes here. Among them, the Green Marine, Blix, Connections, and Almost Spring themes are very popular. Take a look at the WordPress theme-download section. One interesting thing is that all these themes are two-column themes, which is the most popular theme format.

Alex Marine's Theme Browser

Alex Marine is a developer who has spent a lot of time in developing various plug-ins, extending WordPress, and arranging the WordPress theme competition. His "WordPress 1.5 competition" had huge response. He has developed a theme-browser website where you can select any theme from a drop-down box and instantly check the look of that theme. The URL of this theme browser is `http://www.alexking.org/software/wordpress/theme_browser.php`.

The winning themes from this competition are listed as follows:

- Connections
- Rin
- Red Train

The 'Most Creative Design' prize was won by the Head theme. The 'Pixel-Perfect Design' prize was won by the RDC and the FastTrack themes. The 'Most Versatile Design' prize went to the Zen Minimalist, Sharepoint Like, LetterHead, and Man~ja themes. You can see the complete list of winners at `http://managedtasks.com/wpthemes/blog/2005/03/31/the-winners/`.

WRC Theme Browser

There is another theme browser available called the WRC theme browser. This browser also enables you to view the look of every skin, but in a small grid, so you can view more than 16 themes at a time. You can also sort them by different options like one-column themes, multiple-column themes, alphabetically, widget-ready, plug-in required, date of publication, sidebars, etc. This is a very useful option. The URL of this theme browser is `http://themes.wordpress.net`.

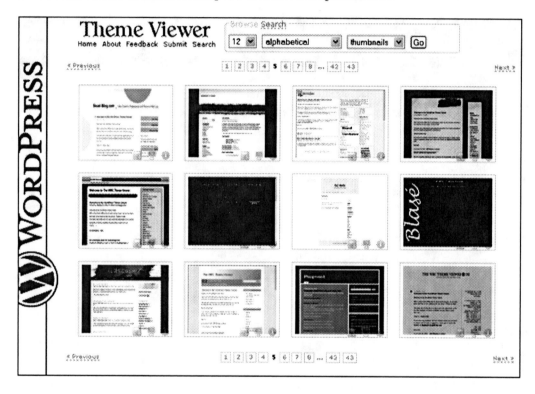

You can also see the list of available files and a small description of the theme when you select it from the list.

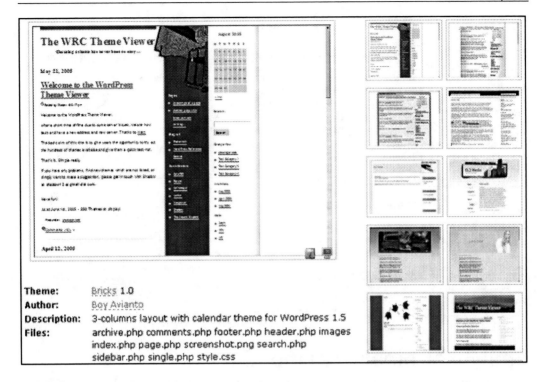

Theme:	Bricks 1.0
Author:	Boy Avianto
Description:	3-columns layout with calendar theme for WordPress 1.5
Files:	archive.php comments.php footer.php header.php images index.php page.php screenshot.png search.php sidebar.php single.php style.css

Central Theme List at Codex

This is the biggest repository of themes for WordPress. It is an editable Wiki where developers can list their themes after release. Codex displays themes under ten major categories like one-column themes, two-column themes, unique themes, widget-ready themes, etc. The URL of this page is `http://codex.wordpress.org/Using_Themes/Theme_List`.

USING THEMES/THEME LIST

DOCUMENTATION

✿ Home Page
✿ WordPress Lessons
✿ Getting Started
✿ Working with WordPress
✿ Design and Layout
✿ Advanced Topics
✿ Troubleshooting
✿ Developer Docs
✿ About WordPress

CODEX RESOURCES

✿ Community portal
✿ Current events
✿ Recent changes
✿ Random page
✿ Help

HOSTED BY

Yahoo Hosting

There are many places online to obtain new themes for WordPress. Here is a short list of themes.

Note: If you add your theme to this list, please verify that your theme will successfully install on a fresh WordPress installation. The link to the Theme must feature a link to the demo and/or screenshots of the various page views and features, and a downloadable file of the Theme. Please add the license under which themes are released and add keyword descriptions to your Theme's listing. For more information on the criteria for inclusion and promotion of your WordPress Theme see Promoting Your Theme. **Themes that do not comply will be removed.**

One Column   [EDIT]

Themes with content only.

And Black Met White
By Tonystreet.com, Simple, One Column, Sidebar at bottom of page, Reminds me of Oreos, Released under GPL.

And Black Met White II
By Tonystreet.com, Very simple, Sidebar uses Blasé Engine, minimalistic, customizable, basic. Released under Creative Commons License

Emily Robbins's Theme List

Emily Robbins is a blogger who has been researching about blogs and blog designs for a long time. She has listed more than 805 themes in her website in different categories. This site is worth looking to search for your desired theme. The URL of her theme list is `http://www.emilyrobbins.com/how-to-blog/comprehensive-list-of-615-free-wordpress-15-and-20-themes-templates-available-for-download-266.htm`.

March 7, 2005

Comprehensive list of 805+ Free WordPress 1.5 and 2.0 Themes / Templates available for download

Updated April 24, 2006

(Last : 04/24/06 - Now listing 807 WordPress Themes available for download!)

Themes which I have tested as also working with WordPress 2.0+ are labeled as: *tested with WordPress 2.0* Those that support sidebar widgets are labeled as: *includes wordpress widgets support*

Note that *most* wordpress 1.5 themes are likely to work with wordpress 2.0 *unless they require specific plugins to work properly* (in which case they'll only work if the required/included plugins ALSO work with wordpress 2.0+)

WordPress 1.5+ uses a system that takes the template to the next level –WordPress themes. Not only are there manyWP themes which are freely available to download and use in your own blog, but you can use Ryan Boren's ThemeSwitcher plugin to allow your weblog visitors to change your blog's theme on the fly (which is pretty darn cool) (and yes, the ThemeSwitcher does work with WordPress 1.5+ even tho it was originally designed for 1.3)

Since I had to search all over the place to try to find WordPress templates (er, themes), I figured I'd save you all the time and maintain a list here of every single WordPress 1.5+ Theme I could find. I also tried to specify the rare WordPress themes with a three

Blogging Pro Theme List

Blogging Pro is a very famous site that delivers news, tips and tricks, and downloadable things for different kinds of blogs. This site also lists WordPress themes sorted date-wise. They review each of these themes manually. It's a great site to check recent themes. You can find the Blogging Pro theme list at `http://www.bloggingpro.com/archives/category/wordpress-themes/`.

Paid Theme List at Template Monster

Template Monster is a site designed especially for amazing web templates and themes. All themes and templates are paid and you can customize themes according to your need. They offer original source files with each of their templates. You can find the Template Monster WordPress theme list at `http://www.templatemonster.com/category/wordpress-themes/`.

Factors to Consider while Choosing a Theme

When you choose a theme, you should consider different factors like the content of your blog, the audience, and the meaning of the colors used. For example, you may see `http://blogs.msdn.com` and `http://googleblog.blogspot.com`. They are simple and elegant. They also serve their content in a formal and concise way so that it's a pleasant experience for all to visit them. This is just an example, but you may have to consider some issues like this while choosing a theme for your site. However, there is nothing to worry about; you need not be a color psychologist or a specialist in user experience. In the following sections, we will discuss some basic factors that should be considered before applying themes to a site.

Content of the Blog

It is a wise saying that "content is the king". Whatever your blog is about, content is at the heart of it. While choosing your theme, please keep a sharp watch on the subject of your content and whether the theme represents all the content that you want to show. Some themes can show static pages, while some can't. When you want to tell something that does not fall under a specific blog category, for example, about you or about your works and projects, that content is considered as static content. Content of this type is represented in separate pages. So when you plan to display static pages, your theme must be capable of showing them. Otherwise, you will add pages through the WordPress administration panel and they will not even be displayed.

Another important part of a theme is a "search" field. In this textbox, users can search for some specific keywords in your blog. Not all themes support searching. So please consider this option while choosing a theme, if you need a search button.

In themes, there must be an available place where you can add your favorite links or blogrolls. Themes must also support an RSS button, both in RSS and Atom format.

A typical theme must support archives where your blog posts are categorized by the date of posting. In WordPress themes, you can display your blog posts categorized by month, week, or date. These categories are called archives. Another important thing that themes should support is the display of available categories to which the posts belong. If a user can see the available category list, it will be easier for him or her to sort out what he or she is looking for.

In every post, a theme must supply a link for trackbacking that post. There must be a place where you can comment on every post.

Themes should also support pagination, which means having a navigation system to go to the previous and next pages. Usually in a WordPress blog, ten posts are shown in each page. So if you want to see previous posts, there must be a way to navigate through them. In the sidebar, many themes can display the latest posts and latest comments. Whenever a single post is displayed, a list of the relevant posts is also displayed in some of these themes.

Another very important issue is that some themes come with an inbuilt horizontal menu or vertical menu. Some of these themes are fine, since they use original contents of your WordPress blog posts, pages, and other stuff to create these dynamic menus. However, most surprisingly many themes come with some sticky content. For example, in some themes there is an option "About the Company" in the horizontal or vertical menu and when someone clicks on it, it redirects to a page that you can never create via the admin panel, or you can supply the contents for those pages. Moreover, it is totally irrelevant for an individual blogger to have a default link "About the Company" in his or her blog. To remove those default menus, you have to modify themes manually and for this programming as well as HTML knowledge is required, which regular, non-tech bloggers may not have.

So while choosing themes, keep your eyes on these factors and judge whether each theme can really represent your content. Besides, keep in mind that people like simplicity. So if your readers are corporate users, try to be simple and precise.

Audience

Although there is no strict rule for choosing themes according to the article type, but if you look around, you may see that the appearance of a theme should match with the age of your audience, their mood, and their style. When you are writing for kids, you should choose something funny or colorful. When you are writing for travelers, your theme color should be green or blue, i.e. the color of nature. Travelers are always colorful, so try to use some bright and shiny themes. If your readers are corporate users, try to be precise while choosing these themes. Use your intelligence while choosing a theme according to the audience.

Colors and Fonts

Colors are also a very important thing when you consider the mood of your audience, and of course they are also relevant to the content of your blog.

Colors can give a very pleasant experience to your user, if you choose them correctly. Be very careful while mixing up different colors, especially for typeface. A very good color for the font may look very odd if the background color doesn't match with it. The colors that you choose for your blog will also determine the readability of your content. Nevertheless, have fun with colors.

Font is another issue to consider while choosing themes. Some fancy themes may use a lot of font faces in a theme, but that really degrades the user experience. Whether it's your own theme or a third-party one, try to use the minimum number of fonts. As far as possible, stay with only one font (size may vary for different sections, like header, footer, etc.) or at the maximum two.

There are some sites that really care about accessibility issues. Some plug-ins are available for switching between font sizes. For example, not all people may feel good with the same font size; these plug-ins give them the facility to increase the font size at run time.

Theme Size

Many of these themes use graphical content. Some of them style their appearance using just CSS, some use both CSS and Images. If you look around some very popular themes like Green Marine, Almost Spring, or Blix, you will notice that they do the styling entirely using CSS; so they are small in size. Connection, another popular theme, uses a banner that is also very small in size. So you must make sure that your theme is small in size, and easy to load for users having slow Internet connections. If you use high-speed broadband connections, size doesn't matter for you. However, the fact is that you are not writing a blog for yourself. There will be readers from around the world where high-speed Internet connection is too costly and they depend on dial-up or slow connections. So if your blog takes minutes after minutes to load, the chance is that the viewer will not feel comfortable and will be unlikely to come back to read it. Choose a theme that is decent, easy to navigate, easy to load, and most importantly comfortable to read through.

Installing and Changing Themes

So far we have learned where to find exciting themes and how to choose them. Now it's time to install themes practically on your WordPress blog. Themes are basically a set of files. Installing a theme is a very easy process. You have to extract the archive and paste the extracted content in a special folder called **themes** inside your WordPress folder. The following steps will guide you through.

Step 1: Download the Theme You Want

Wherever you can find your favorite theme, download it from there.

Step 2: Extract the Content

Now extract the content of that theme file to a folder on your local machine. If you plan to use a web-based FTP client like Net2FTP, then you can skip this step since with Net2FTP you can upload archived files in your FTP server and Net2FTP will automatically extract them if you need.

Step 3: Upload

Now you need to upload the contents that you have extracted from your theme to the **themes** folder of your WordPress blog. For this purpose, you must have an FTP client. You can either use a desktop client (my favorite is Filezilla; it's a free and an open-source program that you can download from

`http://filezilla.sourceforge.net/`), or you can use a web-based FTP client
such as Net2FTP from `http://www.net2ftp.com`.

Uploading via Filezilla

First connect to your FTP server using Filezilla and locate the **wp-content/themes**
folder inside your WordPress folder. Take a look at the following screenshot:

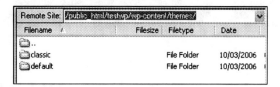

You can see only two themes here; one is **classic** and the other is **default**. WordPress
comes with these two themes by default. Now locate the theme you want to
upload. In the left-hand side pane of Filezilla, you will find the files on your local
machine. For example, I am going to upload the **almost-spring** theme from the
G:\Wp\themes folder.

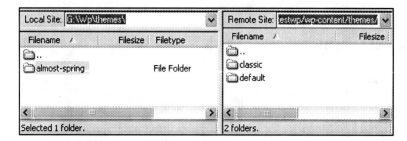

Now drag the theme folder from the left pane to the right pane. It will be
uploaded automatically.

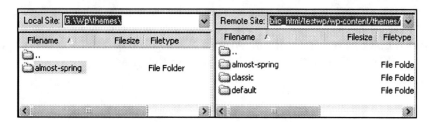

That's it! You are done.

Step 4: Test the Theme

To change the theme and test newly installed themes, you must log into the administration panel. There is a menu named **Presentation** that will help you to change themes for your WordPress installation. Now it's time to test it practically. Log into the administration panel and click on the **Presentation** menu.

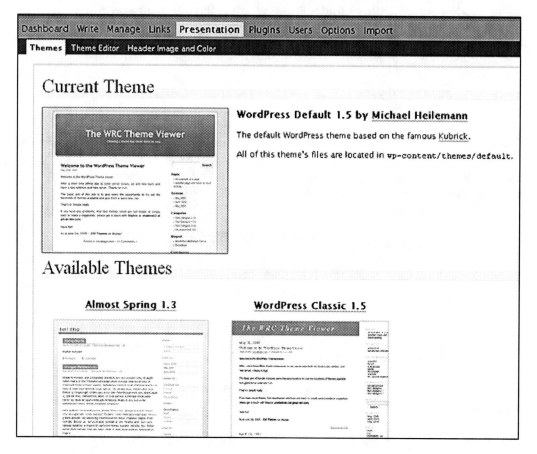

Please notice that our recent addition, **Almost Spring 1.3**, is visible on this page. To change your theme to the desired one, just click on the image.

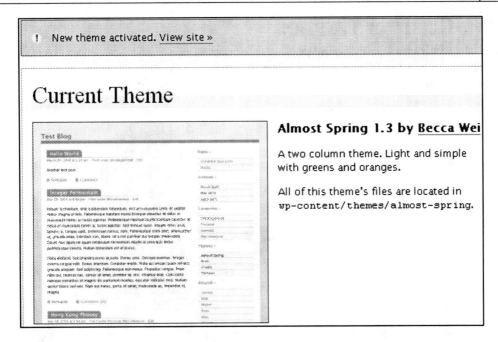

Now Almost Spring is our selected theme. If you browse your WordPress URL now, you will see the change.

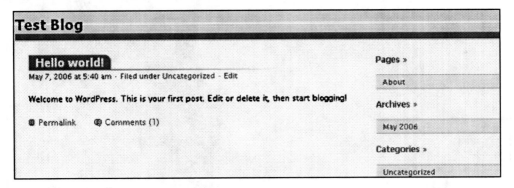

Whenever you add a new theme in the **themes** folder, you will find it in the **Presentation** panel.

Typical Appearance of Different Themes

Here is the appearance of some typical one-column, two-column, three-column, and four-column themes.

One-Column Themes

One-column themes just display posts, and sometimes have a sub-menu at the header and the footer; there is no sidebar. Let us take a look at a typical one-column theme. The theme we display here is **Off The Wall** developed by Sheba Um Malek.

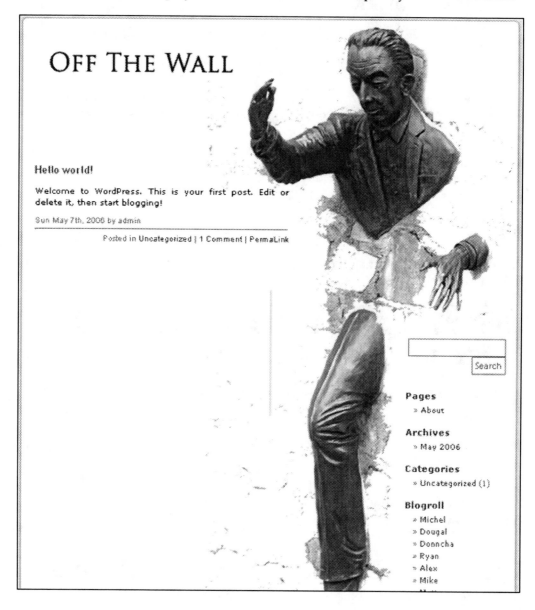

Two-Column Themes

Two-column themes display a column for posts and also a sidebar for displaying other information. For most examples in this chapter, we will use the Almost Spring theme, which is a two-column theme developed by Becca Wei.

Three-Column Themes

Three-column themes display one column for posts, and the other two columns for links. Let us take a look at the "Identification Band Triplet-Centered Boyish Style" theme version 2.0 by Frederic de Villamil aka neuro. You can find his other themes at `http://t37.net/identification-bands`.

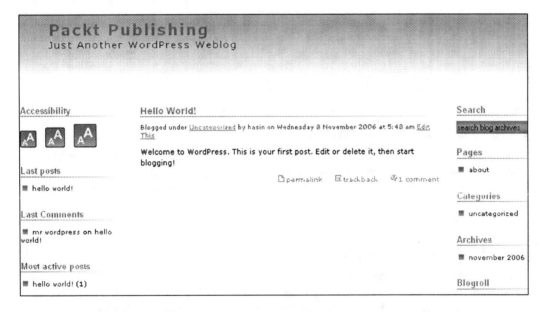

You can choose another flavor for these three-column themes as shown in the following screenshot:

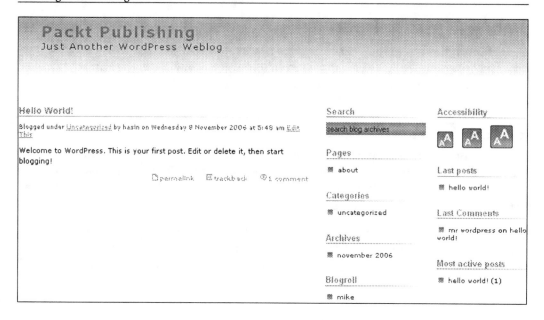

Four-Column Themes

Four-column themes are rare, though there are some very good themes available. These themes display posts in one column and the other three columns are used for different administration tasks. You can find four-column themes at http://fredericdevillamil.com/pages/themes#fourcols.

Some Unique Themes

There are some unique themes available, which enable several administrative panels when installed that are not generally available. Let us take a look at two of them. The first one is Kiwi, a fantastic free theme that can really bring an elegant look to your blog.

You can find Kiwi at http://no.oneslistening.com/. Kiwi is developed by Yas.

Kiwi enables some administrative panels. With Kiwi, you can make any post a featured one. Kiwi also enables you to set some option froms the **Options** menu; you will find it named **Kiwi**.

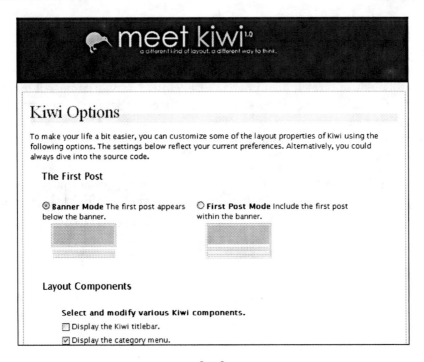

From the post menu, you will also find some options from where you can select any post as a featured post.

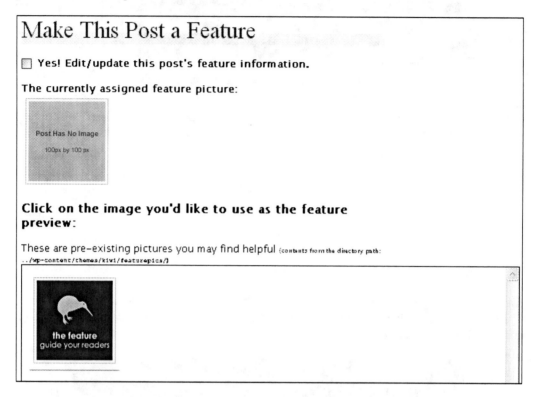

There is another theme that can enable outstanding features for your WordPress blog. This theme is not free for commercial use. However, you can use it for almost any purpose if you like to use it personally. The theme is Semilogic and you can find it at http://www.semiologic.com/software/sem-theme/. The theme will convert your WordPress blog into a manageable CMS. You will have some great features with this theme.

After installing Semilogic, you will find several menus in your administration panel. For example, if you look at your **Presentation** menu, you will find the following:

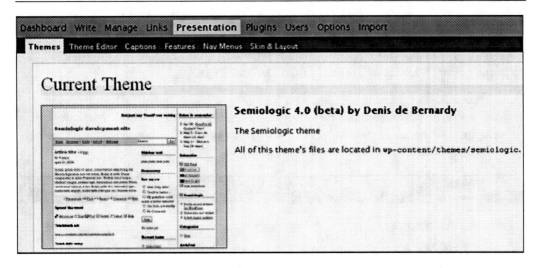

Semilogic enables the following administrative panels under the **Presentation** menu.

Basic Modification

There is no guarantee that themes developed by other people can fully satisfy your requirement. You may need something more that is not available in those themes. So the only way you can achieve that functionality is by developing themes on your own, or by customizing an existing theme. Here we will discuss how to enable and disable some functionality in WordPress themes. We will discuss developing themes yourself in Chapter 7. However, you need some basic PHP knowledge to modify themes for:

- Enabling/disabling the page menu
- Enabling/disabling search in the sidebar
- Enabling/disabling calendar in the sidebar
- Adding static content in the sidebar

Structure of a Theme

Before starting modifications, you should have a proper understanding of the files that are responsible for themes. When a page is rendered, it calls the index.php file in the particular theme folder that is currently set as active. The index file first loads the header, then displays the posts, then loads the sidebar, and finally loads the footer. So for the four basic modifications, we need to modify the file that is responsible for the sidebar. It is usually called `sidebar.php`.

To modify code in these theme files, you will get a separate administration panel under the **Presentation** menu. The sub-menu is called **Theme Editor**. You can edit either using this panel or manually by editing files under the theme folder. For small modifications, the **Theme Editor** is really handy.

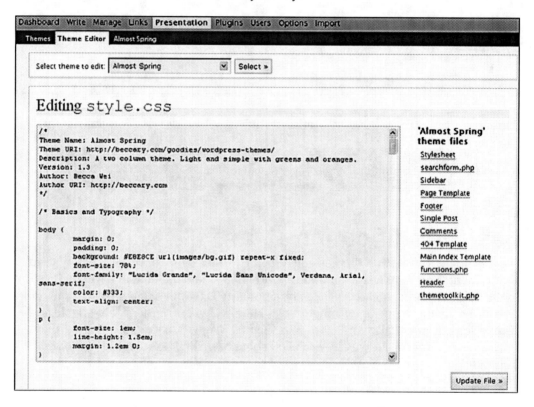

Here you will see the code of the CSS file of the currently selected theme. You will also see all the files in the current theme on the right-hand side pane. If you click on **Sidebar** on the right-hand side, you will see the code of that file.

```
Editing sidebar.php
```

```
</div>

<div id="sidebar">
<ul>
<?php if ( !function_exists('dynamic_sidebar') || !dynamic_sidebar() ) : ?>

        <?php wp_list_pages('title_li=<h2>' . __('Pages') . '</h2>' ); ?>

        <li id="archives">
                <h2><?php _e('Archives'); ?></h2>
                <ul>
                <?php wp_get_archives('type=monthly'); ?>
                </ul>
        </li>

        <?php /* Uncomment this to display the calendar
        <li id="calendar">
                <?php get_calendar(); ?>
        </li>
        */ ?>
```

**'Almost Spring'
theme files**

Stylesheet

searchform.php

Sidebar

Page Template

Footer

Single Post

Comments

404 Template

Main Index Template

functions.php

Header

themetoolkit.php

Enabling/Disabling Page Menu in the Sidebar

If you open the sidebar for editing, using the theme editor or manually, you will find a line where the page menu is rendered. The line is as follows:

```
<?php wp_list_pages('title_li=<h2>' . __('Pages') . '</h2>' ); ?>
```

The function wp_list_pages() displays all the available pages in a list. The parameter Pages is the title of the section. So if you change Pages to anything else, like Navigation, you will notice the change in the theme.

```
<?php wp_list_pages('title_li=<h2>'. __('Navigation').'</h2>' ); ?>
```

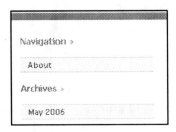

If we remove the code or just comment the line as shown next, the page menu will disappear. Similarly, if there is no page menu in a theme, we can add this line to enable it.

```
<?php //wp_list_pages('title_li=<h2>'. __('Pages').'</h2>' ); ?>
```

Test Blog

Hello world!

May 7, 2006 at 5:40 am · Filed under Uncategorized · Edit

Welcome to WordPress. This is your first post. Edit or delete it, then start blogging!

Permalink   Comments (1)

Archives »

May 2006

Categories »

Uncategorized

Enabling/Disabling Search Bar in the Sidebar

Search is a very useful feature in a WordPress blog. Visitors can search for a specific keyword in your blog. If you don't find any search bar in a theme, you can modify `index.php` (the main index template) to achieve the functionality.

Usually search bars are placed in the sidebar. So if you find the search bar in any other place, for example in the top menu, there is a fairly good chance that it is inside the `header.php` file. In most cases, the search form is placed inside `sidebar.php`. The file that is responsible for displaying search results is `search.php`. If you look at the `index.php` file of the Almost Spring theme, you will find that they include the search bar using a separate `get_sidebar()` function that actually includes `searchform.php`. Inside the search form, you will find the `<form>` element for search.

```
<form method="get" action="<?php echo $_SERVER['PHP_SELF']; ?>">
<p>
<input type="text" value="<?php echo wp_specialchars($s, 1); ?>"
name="s" id="s" />
<input type="submit" value="<?php _e('Search'); ?>" />
</p>
</form>
```

In other themes like Connections, Pool, and Green Marine, this code is embedded in `sidebar.php`. In some themes like Blix, the search form is embedded in `header.php`. You can easily locate the search bar if you analyze the appearance of your theme as well as the `index.php` file.

Let us disable the search bar. All you have to do is just comment the preceding code. In HTML, if you place some code inside `<!--` and `-->` markers, it will be considered as a comment and will not be rendered in the browser. Let us modify the code and make it look as follows:

```
<!--
<form method="get" action="<?php echo $_SERVER['PHP_SELF']; ?>">
```

```
<p>
<input type="text" value="<?php echo wp_specialchars($s, 1); ?>"
name="s" id="s" />
<input type="submit" value="<?php _e('Search'); ?>" />
</p>
</form>
-->
```

Now refresh the blog and you will notice that the search bar has disappeared. If you find the search bar missing in any theme, just add the preceding code at the appropriate place and you will obtain the search bar functionality in your blog.

Enabling/Disabling Calendar in a Theme

If you can display your posts in a calendar, it will be very useful for your visitors. They can jump to posts of any date using this calendar. Let us look at a sample calendar.

This is a sample calendar in WordPress blog. WordPress has built-in functions for generating such a calendar. Please note that the dates on which you made some post, are highlighted and are clickable. For example, in the preceding calendar, you can click on 7th May to go to the post that you made on that day.

To enable the calendar in WordPress themes, just add the following code in `sidebar.php`:

```
<li id="calendar">
    <?php get_calendar(); ?>
</li>
```

Sometimes, in some themes you may need to add the following lines:

```
<ul>
..<li id="calendar">
....<?php get_calendar(); ?>
```

```
..</li>
</ul>
```

That's it!

Adding Static Content in the Sidebar

Usually a sidebar is generated dynamically, with various types of links. If you want to add some static content to the sidebar, open the `sidebar.php` file and add some code like the following:

```
<h2>About Me</h2>
<ul>
<li>
Hi I am Hasin Hayder, You can find my personal blog at <a
href='http://hasin.wordpress.com'>The Storyteller</a>
</li>
</ul>
```

You will see the output as follows:

You can add something very special about you as static content in the sidebar.

Summary

This chapter describes how to manage the outlook of your WordPress blog. You have learned the necessity of themes, and the basic factors to be considered while choosing themes. There are plenty of sources from where you can download themes for your blog.

You also learned how to modify some basic features so that your blog perfectly fits your basic requirements. WordPress is a very popular and customizable blogging engine. So it's not a big matter to achieve great things by making small changes. Just practice these things, and you will discover many interesting features of WordPress by yourself.

In the next chapter, we will show you the details of posting, commenting, and other relevant features of your blog.

4
Blogging your Heart Out

WordPress is a very powerful blogging tool. It is user-friendly and gives you all the necessary tools for successful blogging. So far we have learned the features of a basic blog and the factors to be considered for choosing and installing themes. In this chapter, we are going to see the details of posting, commenting, and other relevant settings.

Posts in Detail

Posts are the main part of a blog. Every article that you publish in your blog will be considered as a post. Usually posts are same as blog entries. So in every blog, posts get the highest focus.

Before starting, you need to know about WYSIWYG (What You See Is What You Get) editors, in which you get the final result looking exactly the same as what you see in the edit box. This is a popular term for editors. In editors like OpenOffice or Microsoft Word, you can do almost everything you want to.

To give the same flexibility while writing in web applications, developers created JavaScript-based WYSIWYG editors. The most popular WYSIWYG editors for the web are HTMLArea editor, FCK editor, and TinyMCE editor. Prior to version 2.0, WordPress had only a plain text editor. Although you can get WYSIWYG editors by installing plug-ins, this is something really big to get a simple job done. In WordPress 2.0, you have both the WYSIWYG editor and the plain text editor bundled together. The TinyMCE editor is set as the default WYSIWYG editor in WordPress 2.0.

Adding Posts to your Blog

Adding posts in WordPress is easy. We have seen the basic how-tos of posting in Chapter 2. In this section, we will go into the details of posting and will learn about rich text editing and how to get some extra jobs done while posting.

After logging into the WordPress control panel, you will find that there are two ways in which you can make a post. You can click on **write a new post** or, you can click on **write** from the menu bar; either way you will reach your posting page. As WordPress features rich text editing, you can do a lot of things with this cool editor. As you write, it will automatically format your text into HTML. Besides rich text editing, you must have some basic knowledge about any markup language like HTML. Let us take a look at the writing environment for your article:

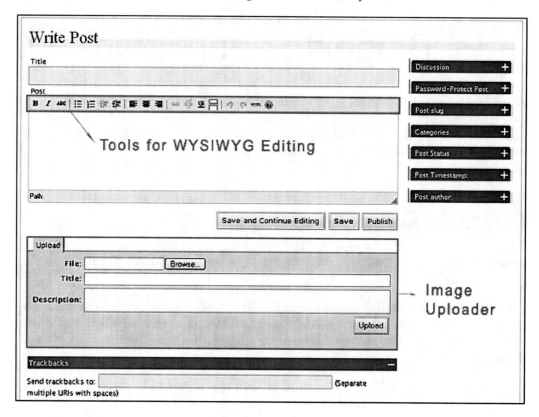

The preceding screenshot is a combined view of the various significant parts of the post editor. Wordpress gives you ultimate control over your content. You can do almost everything with it. Following are the parts visible in the screenshot:

- **Title**: Every post must have a title. This is the first thing that people will see. If the title is interesting, they will go through your content. So you must choose some attractive but relevant title for your post. Don't make it short or cryptic, but rather simple and informative. Another advantage of a good title is that a title with important words will increase the search-engine ranking of your page. Users will get your page easily via search engines if the titles are relevant to what they are looking for.

- **Content**: While writing your content, always use hyperlinks to the key points of your content. This will increase your page rank by generating outgoing requests. For example, if you write a post describing something about WordPress, always make the word "WordPress" hyperlinked to its website `http://www.wordpress.org`. Later in this chapter, we will see how to format your content as rich text. For the time being, just remember that content is something that keeps your site alive and makes it popular.

- **Image uploader**: In WordPress 1.5.x, it was a hassle to add images to your post content. In Wordpress 2.0, this has been simplified by providing this image uploader option. With this option, you can upload as many images as you want. These images will be stored into a basic repository from which you can use and reuse them time after time.

- **Discussion Settings**: With this settings panel, you may or may not permit the viewers of your article to make a comment about your post. You can also allow/disallow anyone to make trackbacks to this post. All these settings are to fight against comment flooding and comment spamming. Comment spam is an advertising technique where spammers post a lot of comments including URLs of their products. Sometimes they create automated scripts that surf from blog to blog and automatically submit comments. Excessive comment spamming is known as comment flooding.

- **Password Protection Settings**: Sometimes you may need to post for a specific audience. You may not want anybody excluding them to see this post. For example, your project manager made some post specific to developers or QA assistants and he may not want it to be visible to others. In such a scenario, you can protect your post with a password. So if anyone knows the password to this post, he or she can read the content. The rest of them can only see the title.

- **Post slug**: A post slug is a keyword that describes your post. So when some tag-crawler crawls through your post, it can understand what your post is all about. Always use relevant keywords to describe your post. This is also extremely useful for posts with long titles. If your WordPress installation has custom URL mapping for post permalinks, the long title might look very odd. So you can write anything as a post slug and your URL will be formatted accordingly. This is also useful for bloggers who blog in Unicode (UTF-8). For example, one of my blog's URL is: `http://hasin.wordpress.com/2006/09/24/%e0%a6%ae%e0%a7%87%e0%a6%98-%e0%a6%a6%e0%a7%87%e0%a6%96%e0%a6%a4%e0%a7%87-%e0%a6%87%e0%a6%9a%e0%a7%8d%e0%a6%9b%e0%a7%87-%e0%a6%95%e0%a6%b0%e0%a7%87-%e0%a6%96%e0%a7%81%e0%a6%ac-%e0%a6%9b%e0%a7%8b%e0%a6/`. I then type "cloud" as post slug and my URL is reformatted as `http://hasin.wordpress.com/2006/09/24/cloud/`.

- **Categories**: When you write your content, don't forget to specify the category it should belong to. You may post articles on different topics like Information Technology, Open-Source, Just about You, and so forth in your blog. So when visitors visit your blog, they can choose their topic of interest. When they click on the Open-Source category, they will see only those posts that you post under the Open-Source category. It will save their time and increase the readability of your blog. So always use categories in your posts.

- **Post Status**: Sometimes you may not be ready to write the whole content at once. You may want to write it part by part or you may plan for future edits. In this case, you may not want to publish your post until you finish writing it. So with these settings you can specify whether your post will be published or saved internally as a draft. You may also want this post to be visible to all the registered members of your blog. You can then publish your post as "private". The **Post Status** option helps you with these settings.

- **Timestamp Settings**: If you want to make a post today but want to show it posted at a previous date, or at a future date (probably you won't want it to), this option will help you to change the date settings specific to that post.

- **Trackbacks**: We discussed a lot about trackbacks in Chapter 1. If you are posting about a topic that is already covered in another blog, then you may ping that blog as a confirmation that your post is relevant to that post. If that user allows trackbacks to his or her post, then immediately after pinging his post, there will be a comment with a link to your post published in his or her post. So trackbacks always increase site ranking by creating incoming links (or simply link exchanges).

- **Post Author Settings**: From the **Post author** section on the right side, you will get a list of all the available users in your blog. If you are the only author of your blog, there is nothing to change. However, if there are multiple authors registered in your blog, then while writing a post you can select any author name from the list and the post will be displayed as posted by that author.

Rich Text Editing

In the post editing page, you will get a WYSIWYG editor for editing the content of your post. WYSIWYG editors are also known as rich text editors. WordPress uses the **TinyMCE** editor as its integrated rich text editor. These editors automatically generate necessary HTML code as soon as you format the content. You don't need to bother about anything else like HTML tags, hyperlinks, images, etc. In this section, we will delve into the rich text editing environment integrated with WordPress.

The following screenshot shows the toolbar that helps you to format your text. Let's see what the tools actually do.

The following three buttons help you to make your text bold, italics, or strikethrough. To see them in action, just select some text inside your editor and click on one of these buttons.

The following four buttons help you to add bullets or numbered bullets, and outdent or indent your text, respectively. You will get the outdent button enabled only when you are inside an indented text block.

The following set of buttons is for justifying your text. By clicking on them, you can make your paragraph left-justified, centered, or right-justified respectively.

If you are not familiar with justifying, let's take a look at the following image to understand what left, center, and right justification are.

The following set of buttons is for justifying your text. By clicking on them, you can make your paragraph left-justified, center-justified, or right-justified respectively

The following set of buttons is for justifying your text. By clicking on them, you can make your paragraph left-justified, center-justified, or right-justified respectively

The following set of buttons is for justifying your text. By clicking on them, you can make your paragraph left-justified, center-justified, or right-justified respectively

In the preceding screenshot, the first paragraph is left-justified, next paragraph is centered, and the last paragraph is right-justified.

The following buttons help you to add a hyperlink or remove an existing hyperlink from your content.

To make any content hyperlinked, select some text that you want to have as a hyperlink and then click on the first button. You will be asked for the URL of the hyperlink. If your URL is an absolute URL to another site or web page, insert the URL followed by some required text. Following is a screenshot while inserting a hyperlink:

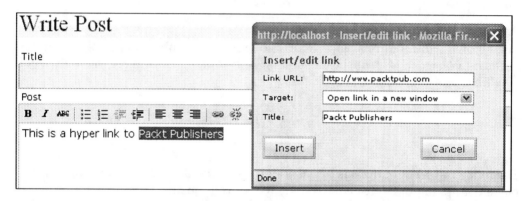

From the hyperlink dialog box, select the window in which the hyperlinked URL will open. You can select either **Open link in a new window** or **Open link in same window** as target; however, the better choice is opening the link in a new window as users can read both your post content and the new URL at the same time. **Title** is the displayable text that you will see when you move your mouse over this hyperlink. To remove a hyperlink, just select the hyperlinked text and click on the second hyperlink button.

Using the following button you can insert an image. Just remember that you can only include an image from an existing URL.

If you want to insert images of your own, you have to use the image uploader that comes later in this chapter. You will get the following dialog box when you click on this button.

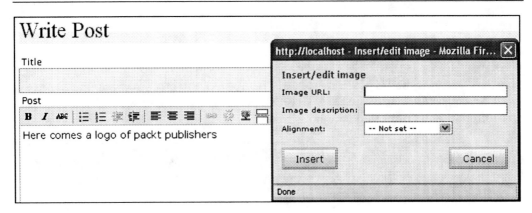

Insert any **Image URL** following the text `http://`, for example
`http://www.packtpub.com/images/logo.jpeg`. **Image description** is the text that
is displayed when the image fails to load. You can use different alignment options
from the **alignment** drop-down box.

If your content is too large, it may not be wise to display all of it on the front page of
your blog. If you do, the blog front page may look ugly and people may lose interest
in reading your blog because they have to scroll down a long post made by you and
then find your next post. It is a better decision to display portions of your post and
add a **Read more** link in your front page under each long post.

After reading the excerpt, if anyone is interested, he or she may click on the **Read
more** link to read the rest of your post. This technique helps to make your blog look
professionally neat and clean. You can display the excerpt up to a marker point in
your post. This marker is `<!--more-->`. If you insert this marker inside your content,
the text before this marker will be considered as the excerpt and displayed on the
front page. The following button inserts the marker when you click on it:

These buttons help you to undo and redo your actions, respectively.

The next button, shown overleaf, is an interesting tool in this rich text editor. I have
already said that rich text editors automatically generate HTML equivalent to your
formatted content. After editing text, you can see its exact HTML code by clicking
this button.

You can even edit the HTML code directly from this code box. Take a look at the following screenshot. The HTML code box shows you the exact HTML code according to your formatted content.

This button shows some necessary help while editing rich text. You will find some great help here.

Shortcuts while Editing

There are several keyboard shortcuts available while editing in the rich text editor. These shortcuts save your time and help you to write your content smoothly without interruption. Let's look at the available **Hotkeys**; you will find them by clicking the help button inside your rich text editor.

Uploading and Using Images in your Post

When you need to upload and use your own images, you have to use the image uploader available within the post section. This uploader helps you to upload images, manage them, and reuse them as many times as you want. You can upload images with all possible extensions like `.jpeg`, `.jpg`, `.png`, `.gif`, `.bmp`, etc. Let us take a closer look at the image uploader.

To upload an image, let's browse for it. Give the image a relevant title and some description that helps you choose the right image from a set of uploaded images. After selecting the image file and inserting a title and a description, click on the **Upload** button.

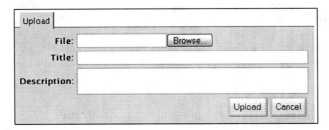

This is the thumbnail of the uploaded image file.

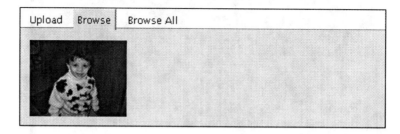

If you click on it, you will see a menu that appears instantly as follows. The first three of these options will change one after another if you click over them. For example, if you click on **Using Thumbnail**, it will display the next active option **Using Original**, and so forth. In this picture, you are just viewing the default options that will change if you click on any of them.

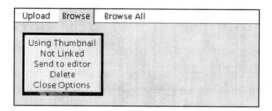

The first option is **Using Original** or **Using Thumbnail**; this is how the image will be displayed in your post content.

The second option is **Not Linked**, **Linked to Image**, or **Linked to Page**. This specifies which action will take place when someone clicks over this image. There are three choices:

- When someone clicks on this image nothing happens (specified by **Not Linked**).

- When someone clicks on the thumbnailed image it shows the original image itself (specified by **Linked to Image**).

- When someone clicks on this image it redirects to the container post (specified by **Linked to page**).

The third option is **Send to Editor**. When you click on it, the image will be inserted into your rich text editor.

The fourth option is to **Delete** the image.

The fifth option is to **Close** the menu.

If you plan to upload more images, then you can traverse through all your uploaded images by clicking on **Browse All**.

You can manipulate any image from this panel.

Managing Post Categories

When you make a post, always try to categorize it for better readability. Users always like to find articles about their interests. So if you categorize your articles, visitors can find them very easily. In this section, we will learn how to create new categories, how to post under one or multiple categories, and how to manage these categories.

In the posting section, there is a small category management panel in which you can name the new category to which the post should belong. There are also different administration panels for these categories. First let's create some categories before making posts via this category-management panel in the posting section. Take a look at the right side of the rich text editor; you will see the following setting panels:

Click on the **+** sign after **Categories**. You will see the category panel instantly as follows:

Well, from this panel you can add new categories but cannot delete them. WordPress has a different category admin panel. You must use that admin panel to do something more with these categories. For now, let's create new categories titled **PHP** and **Programming**. Soon we will post our articles under these categories.

In the text box, type these two categories together separated by a comma and click on the **Add** button. You will see those categories added instantly and checked by default. When a category remains checked, the post belongs to that category.

For now, we will uncheck the **Uncategorized** category. Let us make a small post and see the output.

History of PHP

February 10th, 2006

PHP succeeds an older product, named PHP/FI. PHP/FI was created by Rasmus Lerdorf in 1995, initially as a simple set of Perl scripts for tracking accesses to his online resume. He named this set of scripts 'Personal Home Page Tools'. As more functionality was required, Rasmus wrote a much larger C implementation, which was able to communicate with databases, and enabled users to develop simple dynamic Web applications. Rasmus chose to » release the source code for PHP/FI for everybody to see, so that anybody can use it, as well as fix bugs in it and improve the code.

By the winter of 1998, shortly after PHP 3.0 was officially released, Andi Gutmans and Zeev Suraski had begun working on a rewrite of PHP's core. The design goals were to improve performance of complex applications, and improve the modularity of PHP's code base. Such applications were made possible by PHP 3.0's new features and support for a wide variety of third party databases and APIs, but PHP 3.0 was not designed to handle such complex applications efficiently.

Posted in PHP, Programming Language | Edit | No Comments »

Take a look at the bottom of this post. It displays the categories under which this article has been posted. Notice the **PHP** and **Programming Language** categories there. If you have many posts under one category, then clicking on that category will display all the posts under that specific category. Another noticeable thing here is that since you are logged in as admin, there is an **Edit** link available to you. If you click on this link, you can edit this post instantly. Other general users will not get this **Edit** link.

You can make a post under as many categories as you want. However, always try to be precise. Don't use too many categories for a single post as that may extremely bother your viewers.

Let us manage categories via the category admin panel. Click on the **Manage** link on the main menu bar and then click on **Categories** on the sub-menu bar.

Categories (add new)

ID	Name	Description	# Posts	Action	
1	PHP		3	Edit	Default
2	Programming Language		0	Edit	Delete
3	Uncategorized		0	Edit	Delete

Note:
Deleting a category does not delete posts from that category, it will just set them back to the default category **PHP**.

Add New Category

Name:

Category parent:

None

Description: (optional)

Here you see a set of tools and a list of all your categories. You can also see how many posts are there in each category and you can even edit or delete them. In the lower section of this page, there is a detailed panel for adding categories. Here **Name** is the title of the category. Through the **Category Parent** field, you can specify whether the new category is a sub-category of a previously created category, or is an independent category. You can also write some description of this category, which will be visible when someone moves the mouse cursor over this category. If you want to place a category as a child of an existing one, just select the parent category from the drop-down box of the **Category Parent** field.

If a post belongs to only one category and you delete that category, then the post will go by default to the **Uncategorized** category.

Managing Existing Posts

We have already seen that when you are logged in as Admin, you can see the **Edit** link just below the article that was posted by you. You can directly edit your post from there. There are separate admin panels for managing your posts. To start managing your posts, just click on the **Manage** button from the menu bar and then click on **Post** from the sub-menu bar.

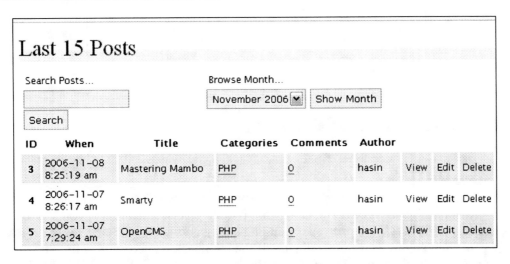

You can view, edit, and delete any post from this panel. If you have a lot of posts, then you can select the month from the **Browse Month** drop-down box and select the posts made in that month only. This will help you find specific posts easily.

The admin panel also helps you to find comments made under any post. You can then read and modify them. We will discuss this option later in this chapter.

Protecting Posts with a Password

In the settings panel, there are password protection settings. With help of this panel, you can protect your posts with a password. Someone can only view your post if he or she knows your password. Let us take a look at the password settings panel:

You can access password protection settings while composing a new post or from the post management panel. From the **Manage** menu, click on **Post**. To protect your post, just type a password and click on the **save** button under the rich text editor. Let us take a look at a protected post.

Protected: History of PHP
February 10th, 2006

This post is password protected. To view it please enter your
password below:

Password: [_____] [Submit]

Posted in PHP, Programming Language | Edit | Enter your password to
view comments

To see this post, just enter the password and hit **Submit**.

Trackbacks

When someone in another blog makes a post on some specific topic and you also
want to make a post in your blog using that remote post as a reference, you can use
trackbacks. Trackback is a process of pinging a blog and telling it that you referred to
a post of that blog in your personal blog. If the trackback is successful, a link to your
blog post will be displayed as a comment in that remote post. The trackbacked blog
engine will crawl through your post and make a link available to its index.

There are some popular pinging services available on the Internet, which index
millions of blogs everyday and archive their content so that users can search through
these contents and go to that appropriate blog post. To name a few, we have
Technorati (`http://www.technorati.com`), Weblogs (`http://www.weblogs.com`),
Feedburner (`http://feedburner.com`), and Feedster (`http://feedster.com`)
among others.

These indexing services are so popular and powerful that they index millions of
blogs everyday. However, these crawlers crawl at a regular time interval. So if you
make a post today and the crawlers crawl to your blog after two weeks, people will
get your post in these indexing services two weeks after your making that post,
which is often quite bothering. For this reason, these indexing services expose some
trackback URLs to which these crawlers are listening. If someone 'knocks' or 'pings'
with an URL, these crawlers immediately crawl to that page and index that post.

An automated pinging mechanism will ping these trackbacks instantly when you
make a post. This will increase your site ranking by making your post visible to all
the people who are searching. Technorati is a popular indexing service. It provides
trackbacks, that you can use for automatic pinging. Let us see the process.

Firstly, go to `http://www.technorati.com` and look at the lower section of the page
to find the **Ping Us** link.

Clicking on this link you will reach the following page:

Ping Us

Updated your site recently? Let us know! Just enter the URL of your blog home page below to get into the Technorati high-priority indexing queue.

URL: [_____] [Ping!]

Automate this! You can have your blog software ping for you. Enter `http://rpc.technorati.com/rpc/ping` into your weblog tool's configuration for Pings and Notifications. Check our **ping configuration page** for more information.

« Technorati Home

Now all you have to do is submit the URL of your blog. The Technorati crawler is familiar with different types of blog engines like WordPress, MT, Blogger, and so on. It will instantly index your site and list the new updates.

Another thing that you can do is, whenever you make a post, just enter the Technorati ping URL `http://rpc.technorati.com/rpc/ping` in the lower portion of your post page, which is called Trackbacks. Take a look at the following screenshot:

If you paste this trackback link in the trackback section, then after submitting the post WordPress will ping Technorati.

However, doing these things manually every time is a hassle. So let us make it automatic so that whenever you make a post, WordPress will ping Technorati. For that purpose log into your admin panel, click on the **Options** tab, and then click on **Writing**.

On the lower portion of this page, you will find a section titled **Update Service**. You may see something like `http://rpc.pingomatic.com/` available there. Ping-O-Matic is a relay ping service that pings many other pinging services automatically. So when you ping Ping-O-Matic, it will do the rest of the job for you.

Let us add the Technorati ping URL `http://rpc.technorati.com/rpc/ping` here. Technorati is a very popular blog-indexing service and if you have your blog listed here, you can expect better page ranking for sure. On the other hand, Ping-O-Matic is a central pinging service that itself pings many other popular services. You just need to add this address in a new line and save it. Your **Update Service** section should look like the following screenshot:

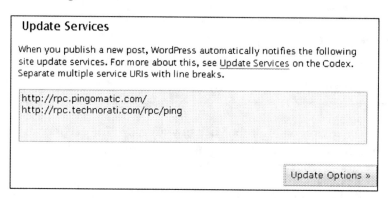

After updating this setting, WordPress will automatically start pinging Technorati and will help to increase your site ranking.

You can also ping other blogs via the available trackback URL under each blog post. However, since it could be misused as a spamming tool, there are plug-ins available to stop trackback spam. One of the most popular ones is Akismet. Akismet is available in both free and commercial editions. To use Akismet, you must have an Akismet 'key' that is available by registering for a free account in WordPress.com.

If you are not sure where to find your Akismet key, create an account in WordPress. com and the API key will be mailed to you when your registration is successful. However, you can actually retrieve it anytime by clicking on the **My Profile** link in the top right corner of your WordPress administration panel. To get your API key, click on that link and you will find your key on the right side. To enable Akismet, you must copy that key and go to the **Plugin** section. After activating the plug-in, it will prompt you for activating Akismet by entering the API key. You can also go to this activation page from this URL:

```
http://your_wordpress_blog/wp-admin/plugins.php?page=akismet\
akismet.php
```

Now paste the key that you copied from your profile page and click on **Save**. That's it!

Here is a comprehensive list of major ping services. You may try with these for better results:

```
http://api.feedster.com/ping
http://api.my.yahoo.com/RPC2
http://ping.blo.gs/
http://ping.feedburner.com
http://ping.syndic8.com/xmlrpc.php
http://pingoat.com/goat/RPC2
http://rpc.blogrolling.com/pinger/
http://rpc.icerocket.com:10080/
http://rpc.pingomatic.com/
http://rpc.technorati.com/rpc/ping
http://rpc.weblogs.com/RPC2
```

Other Useful Settings

While posting, there are some other useful settings available to you. The most important among them is the ability to save a post for later use. You can save a post as a draft from the **Post Status** panel. We have already discussed a little about this panel at the beginning of this chapter. For now, let us take a look at this panel:

To save any post as a draft, just select the **Draft** option and click on **Save**. You may wonder how to get access to these drafts that you had saved earlier. Well, when you log in and come to this **Post** page, you will get all your available drafts at the top of this page. You can also get access to the available drafts by clicking on the **Manage** menu and then the **Post** sub-menu. Take a look at how these drafts are available to you:

To edit a draft, just click on it. To publish a draft, click on it and when it is available in the editing mode, click on the **Publish** button just under the rich text editor.

From the settings panel, you can also manually change the time of your post from the **Post Timestamp** panel. This panel looks like the following:

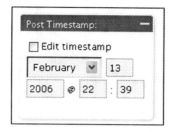

You can select the date and time from here. These settings will override the actual posting date and time for this post.

Posting by Email

Besides the regular style of posting, WordPress also supports different ways of doing this job. For example, you can make posts by mailing to a specific account. This is possible if you set up an email account and make it available to WordPress. For posting by email, let us follow these steps.

Click on the **Options** menu and then **Writing** from the sub-menu.

At the bottom of this page, there is a section titled **Writing by e-mail**. You have to configure some settings before you can start posting by email.

In this section, you have to provide the **Mail server**, **Login name** (usually, that is your full email address), and the **Password**. Finally, select the category to which these posts should go. That's it, you are done!

Remember that whatever you send to this email address, it will be posted to your blog. So don't use your frequently used email address or your public email address. Set up a private (and very private) email address for this purpose. Name the email address quite cryptically. WordPress helps you by providing some cryptic names; look at the portions outlined in the preceding screenshot.

When you send an email, you must tell WordPress that "*I have sent an email, so go and fetch it, and then post it*"; otherwise, WordPress will not know about your email. So immediately after sending an email to this address, access the following URL `http://your_blog_address/wp-mail.php` using your browser. Then WordPress will connect to this email address, fetch the email, and then post it automatically.

If you want to automate this task, you can run this URL automatically via a cron job. In Linux, just set the `cron` command as `php full/path/to/the/wp-mail.php`. Then it will automatically run the script at regular intervals and fetch the emails.

To set up cron jobs, you can access **Cron Jobs** in cPanel. If you have shell access, you can access it by invoking the `crontab -e` command.

For your information, the subject of your email will be considered as the title of the post and the body will be considered as the content. The basic HTML tags will be stripped out.

Other Ways of Posting

There are several other ways of posting in your WordPress blog. WordPress and other standard-compliant blogs implement some standard APIs to complete some specific tasks. There are three popular standard APIs available for blog engines; they are MovableType, MetaWeblog, and Blogger API. If any blog engine implements these APIs, then using standard interfaces, any remote program will be able to manipulate blogs by editing posts, retrieving posts, and so forth under a proper authentication scheme. There are many standard-compliant desktop editors available, which will help you to post on your blog. With these editors you can work faster.

WordPress XML-RPC server implements the following methods:

- `system.multicall`
- `system.listMethods`

- system.getCapabilities
- weblogUpdates.ping
- demo.addTwoNumbers
- demo.sayHello
- pingback.extensions.getPingbacks
- pingback.ping
- mt.publishPost
- mt.getTrackbackPings
- mt.supportedTextFilters
- mt.supportedMethods
- mt.setPostCategories
- mt.getPostCategories
- mt.getRecentPostTitles
- mt.getCategoryList
- metaWeblog.getUsersBlogs
- metaWeblog.setTemplate
- metaWeblog.getTemplate
- metaWeblog.deletePost
- metaWeblog.newMediaObject
- metaWeblog.getCategories
- metaWeblog.getRecentPosts
- metaWeblog.getPost
- metaWeblog.editPost
- metaWeblog.newPost
- blogger.deletePost
- blogger.editPost
- blogger.newPost
- blogger.setTemplate
- blogger.getTemplate
- blogger.getRecentPosts
- blogger.getPost
- blogger.getUserInfo
- blogger.getUsersBlogs

The methods that start with mt are part of the MovableType API, those with blogger are part of the Blogger API, and those with metaWeblog are part of the MetaWeblog API. Among these, MetaWeblog and Blogger API are the most often used.

If you don't understand how these methods work, let's see the following example. For this, you need some basic knowledge about XML-RPC with PHP. To make the following code work, download the PHP XML-RPC package from `http://phpxmlrpc.sourceforge.net/`. Then extract all files from this archive and copy them from the **lib** folder to the directory where you place the following script:

```php
<?php
include("xmlrpc.inc");
$c = new xmlrpc_client("/xmlrpc.php", "hasin.wordpress.com", 80);
$content['title']="XMLRPC Post";
$content['description']="Some content posted using MetaWeblog API";
$content['categories'] = array("frontpage");
$x = new xmlrpcmsg("metaWeblog.newPost",
                    array(php_xmlrpc_encode("1"),
                    php_xmlrpc_encode("admin"),
                    php_xmlrpc_encode("root"),
                    php_xmlrpc_encode($content),
                    php_xmlrpc_encode("1")));
$c->return_type = 'phpvals';
$r =$c->send($x);
if ($r->errno=="0")
echo "Successfully Posted";
else {
   echo "There is some error";
   echo "<pre>";
   print_r($r);
   echo "</pre>";
?>
```

Save this file as `blogapi.php` in any web server (even in your localhost) and browse this page from your browser. After executing this script, log into your WordPress panel and check that there is a new post titled **XMLRPC Post** under the **frontpage** category.

You can play with the other methods as well.

Bookmarklet

Bookmarklet is another interesting feature available with WordPress that enables you to post while you are visiting any page and want to make a quick post with reference to that page. For example, you are browsing an interesting web page under the Packt Publishing website whose URL is `http://packtpub.com/smarty/book` and its title is **Smarty PHP Template Programming**. Now you want to make a new post in your blog with a link to this page. Bookmarklet helps you to do this with the help of a toolbar button.

To enable WordPress bookmarklet in your browser, just log into the admin panel. After clicking on the **Writing** panel, scroll down to the bottom and you will find something as follows:

Please notice that there is a link called **Press it – The Storyteller**, where **The Storyteller** is my blog title. So all you have to do is drag this link to your bookmarklet toolbar. You will see a new button added in the toolbar instantly.

Now when you visit any website and want to post about it, just hit this button and see that the link and the title of that web page is included in your blog post. Take a look at the following screenshot. While visiting the Packt Publishing website, I just hit the button and the screenshot tells the rest.

So you see that after pressing the bookmarklet button, you are redirected to your WordPress posting panel with a link to that page; this is just like inserting a link.

For those who are interested to know the JavaScript code of that bookmarklet button, right-click over it and you will find it. The code is as follows:

```
javascript:
if(navigator.userAgent.indexOf('Safari') >= 0)
{
  Q=getSelection();
}
else
{
  Q=document.selection?document.selection.createRange().
  text:document.getSelection();
}
  location.href='https://hasin.wordpress.com/wp-admin/post-new.php?te
xt='+encodeURIComponent(Q)+'&popupurl='+encodeURIComponent(location.
href)+'&popuptitle='+encodeURIComponent(document.title);
```

Comments in Detail

Comments are a very important part of your blog. User comments always inspire you and give you feedback about your post. However, comments could be misused as a tool for spamming and advertising, which is bothering every blogger. So you must have some knowledge on how to make your blog free from comment spam and make it function smoothly.

How to Make a Comment

If you visit a post, you will notice the **No Comments** or **# Comments** (where # is the total number of comments posted) links just below the post. To make a comment, you can just click on it and go ahead. However, you may not get a comment-writing section all the time, especially if the author of a post disables comments.

If you are logged in as a user of this blog, you can see your name by default as the name of the commenter. However, if you are an outsider, you will see the following section while making comments:

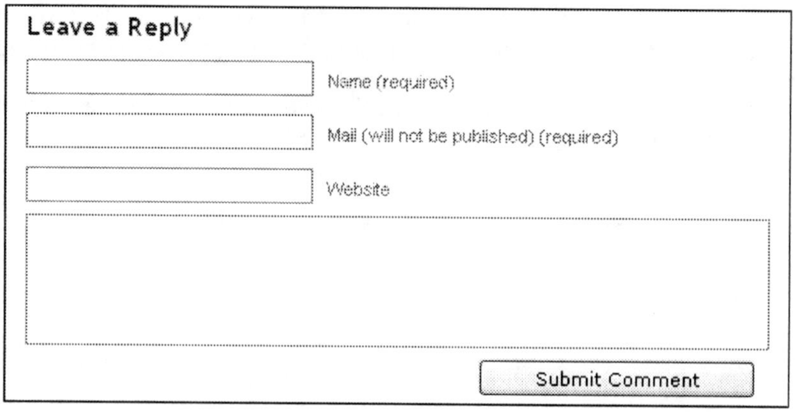

Leave a Reply

Name (required)

Mail (will not be published) (required)

Website

Submit Comment

As you can see, your name and email address are required and your website is optional. However, when you post comment as an outsider (or even as a user sometimes) your comment may not be visible instantly after posting. If the author wants to moderate the comments first, it will be queued to the comment moderation list. It will be displayed after the administrator approves it.

Comment Settings

By default, comments are allowed to publish instantly. However, to prevent spam or to avoid blacklisted comments, we should turn on moderation. Let us see how we can turn on moderation of comments.

Log into the WordPress admin panel, select the **Options** menu, and then click on the **Discussion** sub-menu.

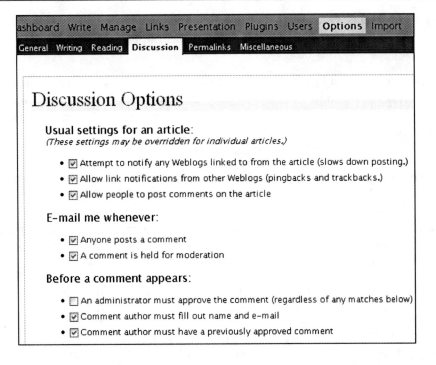

There are different settings for comment administration. The sixth checkbox from the top, which is labeled **An administrator must approve the comment (regardless of any matches below)** is the point we are looking for. If you check this checkbox and save, all comments will be queued for moderation. Let us check it and save.

Now when outsiders post comments in your blog, they will wait for approval. To test it, log out from your admin panel and make a comment on any of your posts.

Let us get familiar with the other options in this page.

Attempt to notify any Weblogs linked to from the article (slows down posting.) indicates that when you make a post, if that post contains hyperlinks, WordPress will try to ping those links. This is to increase the page ranking of your blog. Allowing this one is good for your blog, but it may slow down the posting process a bit as stated. However, it is recommended to keep it checked.

Allow link notifications from other Weblogs (pingbacks and trackbacks.) means that anyone can trackback to your posts and their links will be visible as trackbacks under your posts, as comments. This is also good for increasing the page ranking because it generates an outgoing link to someone else's site; a sort of link exchange. However, this will also increase the tendency of link spam. Bad people can make trackbacks to publish their link on your site, which will act as an advertisement for their site and increase traffic to their site.

Allow people to post comments on the article means whether people can comment on your posts or not. If you uncheck it, the comment option will not be available to anyone; not good for your blog.

E-mail me when anyone posts a comment means WordPress will mail you when someone makes a comment in your blog and that comment is not considered as a spam or is held for moderation. If you turn this on, you will get notification instantly when comments are made. However, if you get huge numbers of comments, this may flood your inbox with lots of notifications everyday.

E-mail me when a comment is held for moderation means when someone makes a comment and that comment is queued for moderation, WordPress will mail you instantly. This setting is quite useful if you enable comment moderation so that you get instant notification and take necessary steps. Please remember that enabling this option as well as the previous one will send you only one mail when a spam is posted, because it already fulfills the first criterion.

Comment author must fill out name and e-mail means what it states. While commenting, name and email fields are mandatory, if you turn this on.

Comment author must have a previously approved comment means if you turn on this setting, comments will not be displayed until the same poster has one approved comment already. However, this setting is not so helpful. If you don't moderate comments, this setting may come handy.

Well, that's it. Let us now start moderating comments.

Comment Moderation

To moderate queued comments, just log into your WordPress admin panel and click on the **Manage** menu and then **Posts**. If you have comments awaiting moderation, you will see something like this:

Taking a closer look at the screenshot, you will see that there is a sub-menu stating that a comment is waiting for moderation. Click on the **Awaiting Moderation (1)** sub-menu. You will see the following screen:

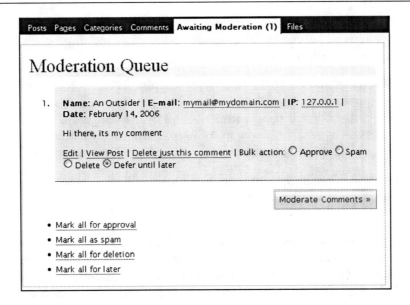

You see that someone named **An Outsider** posted a comment in your blog. If you want to know under which post he or she made this comment, click on the **View Post** link just below the comment. If you want to allow this comment, click on **Approve** and then click on the **Moderate Comments** button. If you feel that you need to edit something in this comment, click on the **Edit** link and you can edit it.

There are four choices for this comment. You can **Approve** it for display. You can mark this comment as **Spam** so that WordPress understands that these sort of comments will be marked as spam in future. You can straight **Delete** it. Finally, if you are not sure what to do with this comment, keep it in the moderation queue for later review by clicking **Defer until later**.

If you have more than one comment, then approving one after another may consume too much time. So there are options for bulk action. On the lower section of this page, there are four links titled **Mark all for approval, Mark all as spam, Mark all for deletion**, and **Mark all for later**. If you click on any one of them, all the comments awaiting moderation and visible in this page will be checked in that category. This will save some time and avoid repetitive task.

Fighting with Comment Spams

You have already got an idea how people can misuse some very useful features of a blog engine, like trackbacks and comments, for advertising purposes and spamming. So all you have to do is start fighting with spams. No doubt, it's very tough to make some automated programs or routines that can detect something as spam because spams don't always fall into a specific category. Moreover, spammers are also clever. They are using new techniques, patterns, and styles for spamming. So it's really tough to automate the process of anti-spamming.

However, all you can do is help the inner anti-spam procedure of WordPress by providing some specific keywords that are generally marked as spam. If you supply these words to WordPress, comments will be marked as spam when they contain any of these words. You have two choices; you can either delete these spams automatically or hold them in the moderation queue for manual checkup.

Let us learn how you can supply these words for WordPress. Go to the **Options** menu and then the **discussion** sub-menu.

Firstly, you will see a section titled **Comment Moderation**. In this section, you can insert suspicious words. If any of these words is found in a comment, WordPress will hold it in the moderation queue, even if you turn on public commenting. There is also another marker to suspect a comment as spam. A comment spam always contains a link, sometimes more than one. In the comment moderation section, there is a box that also detects a comment as spam if a comment contains more than **2** hyperlinks. You can set this number to any valid number. For example, you can queue all comments that contain even one hyperlink.

Comment Moderation

Hold a comment in the queue if it contains more than 2 links. (A common characteristic of comment spam is a large number of hyperlinks.)

When a comment contains any of these words in its content, name, URI, e-mail, or IP, hold it in the moderation queue: (Separate multiple words with new lines.) Common spam words.

Check past comments against moderation list

Comment Blacklist

This is a list of words that you want completely blacklisted from your blog. Be very careful what you add here, because if a comment matches something here it will be completely nuked and there will be no notification. Remember that partial words can match, so if there is any chance something here might match it would be better to put it in the moderation box above.

☑ Blacklist comments from open and insecure proxies.

Further down, there is another section titled **Comment Blacklist**. If you insert some words and WordPress finds any of those words in any comment, then WordPress will delete that comment immediately. Those comments will not be queued even for moderation. So be sure before inserting any words here. Partial words can match here. For example, if you indicate **blackjack** as a blacklisted word and insert only **black** in the comment, then all comments containing the word **black** (black is a common word and there may be many non-spam comments with this word) will be deleted. Moreover, if the word black is part of a word like "blackbox", it will also get deleted. So always be sure before inserting a word in this box.

There is also a checkbox **Blacklist comments from open and insecure proxies** at the lower portion in this page. Comment spams are relayed by open proxies to avoid IP bans. WordPress has an internal list of these open proxies. So if you turn this checkbox on, it will delete any comment made from those blacklisted proxies as well.

Gravatar

When someone makes a comment in your posts, you can see only his or her name. Any person posting comments using your email address must be you. So in whichever blog you make comments using an email address that belongs to you, it indicates that the person who made those comments is you. So an email address is a unique ID of a person.

When someone makes a comment in WordPress, by default you can only see his or her name and email address. It will be more pleasing if you can see his or her avatar in this comment. An avatar is a small image chosen by someone as his or her picture. It may be an image of anything. However, usually a person uses as an avatar a picture that he or she thinks best represents himself or herself.

Gravatars came from this idea. **Gravatar** means "Globally Recognized **Avatar**". www.gravatar.com is mainly a site that hosts your avatar as a URL from its site. You can upload your avatars into the gravatar website and get an ID against your email account. You can change your avatar anytime. You can also rate your gravatar for different audiences like "G" or "R" as suitable to all.

When someone who has an account in gravatar against his/her email address makes a comment in a blog, the blog engine searches the gravatar repository with his or her email address and finds the avatar. Then that blog engine displays the avatar (or gravatar) in every comment he or she has made in the blog.

This is a fantastic feature for every blog engine. Gravatars are known worldwide and almost all the big blog engines have the capability to include this feature. From the gravatar site, there are plug-ins available to add this feature to different blog engines. There is also a plug-in for adding this feature to WordPress.

Summary

The key features of a blog are posts and comments. In this chapter, we learned all about posts and comments. We also learned how to increase the blog rating by using trackbacks. Besides this, we have seen how to fight with comment spammers and comment flooders. We will learn the details about templates, plug-ins, and some core coding parts of WordPress in the upcoming chapters. Till then, happy blogging!

5
Non-Blog Content

WordPress is a powerful content management system, which you can use for building general websites for your organization. A typical website consists of several pages and sometimes some special services like payment processing, RSS, forums, shoutbox, etc. In WordPress, you can do almost everything with the help of several plug-ins. You can also develop a general-purpose website by developing pages, which are basically considered as non-blog content. Before developing a site for your company or product, you may need to plan the site structure; otherwise, the site may look quite messy.

In this chapter, we are going to develop a general website that serves as a showcase for a production company. As a sample, we will develop a website for Packt Publishing, where it will display its books for sale and accept feedback from readers. Let's decide the goal of this site, and then we will proceed towards the site structure.

Goals and Site Structure

We are going to design a website for a publishing company. These sites have some specific goals to fulfill. For example, in our site we will be delivering the following content. However, in real life, a publishing site must also have payment-processing options besides these listed options:

- About page
- Homepage, where visitors get the latest news
- Books page
- Search box
- A page for authors
- Navigation panel
- Top-ranked book list
- An image gallery

Our site has a front page where we will display our latest events. From this page, users will be able to navigate to the book gallery. They can also visit our top-ranked books, where we rank our books based on the hit counts. There must be a page that describes our company, and a page for authors to help them kick-start writing their book with our company.

In our book gallery page, visitors will be able to search books on different criteria. For example, they can sort them by the date of publishing, topics, alphabetically, or by price. From this page, they can click over any book for a detailed description.

A search option must be present so that users can search for books on any topic. They must be able to search by author name, book title, or any specific keyword.

A list of top-ranked books must be present in our front page. You may wonder how we calculate the top-ranked books. For the sake of simplicity, we will calculate the top-ranked books by counting the number of times they have been visited. As each book has its own page (to count hits), we will be able to achieve this functionality. However, in real life there may be several other measures on which the book rank is calculated; for example, the quantity of sales, quantity of positive feedbacks, and quantity of reviews. Among these, hit count is also a reliable process. If people are not interested in your book, definitely your book will receive a relatively lower count of hits compared to other books.

In the front page, we will also provide links to some sites that we think should be displayed there. A calendar must also be present for easier navigation by displaying daily or weekly posts as links in it, so that you can easily find them.

Getting Started

The only way we can create a new book entry is making a post. Then we can sort books according to different criteria.

Making the Site

Now it's time to find a suitable theme for our site. Green Marine always delivers a nice look and feel to your site; so let us try with Green Marine for the time being. We need to modify the functionality of this theme to meet our requirements. There will be small changes that you will have to make and you don't need to be a PHP coder for that.

Our first task is to add some pages where we need less modification. We will add the front page, the about us page, and the author page. Keep in mind that our front page will be a regular WordPress page that excludes the post, which will display only some specific content that we want to display on the front page.

In general, all posts come to the front page instantly. However, in our site we are planning to display only some specific posts. There is no built-in option for this purpose, so we need to modify our theme. These are very small modifications and you don't need to be a regular PHP developer for that.

Step 1: Create a Special Category

From the previous chapter, you have learned how to create categories and how to make some post under a category. To solve our problem, we need to create a category that we will use only for some selected posts to be displayed on the front page. Let us create a category **frontpage** in our blog. You can follow these steps for creating a category:

- Log into the WordPress administration panel.
- Click on the **Manage** menu, and select **Categories**.
- Scroll down to the **Add New Category** section.
- Give the category name as **frontpage** and click on **Add Category**. Please note that it is a top category with no parent. You may add an optional description for each and every category.

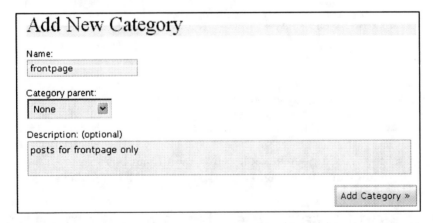

Step 2: Make Some Posts under this Category

After creating the category **frontpage**, add some posts and select **frontpage** as their category from the right-hand side of the post section. Please be sure that your post belongs to this category only.

Now it's time to add some general posts. For this, create another category **book** and make some posts under that **book** category.

If you look at your blog, you will find all the posts from all categories displayed on the front page. However, according to our requirement we will display only specific posts under the **frontpage** category. So we need to modify our theme a bit and tell WordPress to collect those posts only.

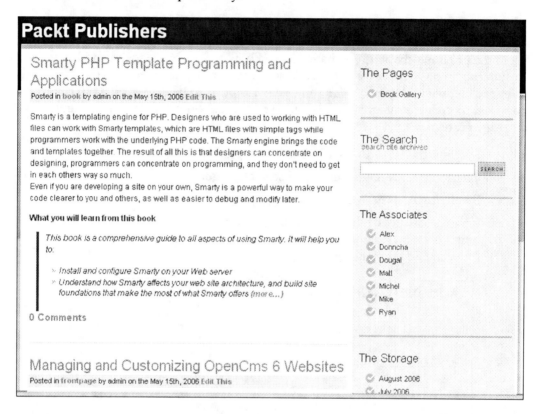

If you look at the preceding screenshot, you will find that posts from all the categories (here **book** and **frontpage**) are displayed on the index page.

Step 3: Modify Main Index Template of the Theme

Using any FTP client or the built-in **Theme Editor**, open the index.php page of your theme for editing. As we are using Green Marine, you will find this file in the path wp-content/themes/greenmarine/index.php.

If you are not sure about the **Theme Editor**, it's accessible as a sub menu under the **Presentation** menu. From the **Theme Editor**, you will find a list of files in the current selected theme that are editable from here, but they must have write permission.

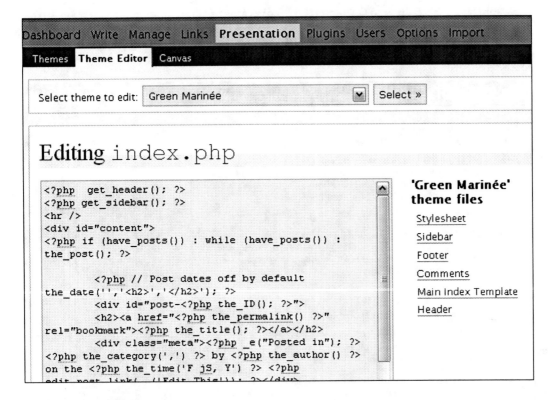

Add the following line just before the `<?php if (have_posts()) : while (have_posts()) : the_post(); ?>` line:

```php
<?php if (is_home())
{
  query_posts("category_name='frontpage'");
}
?>
```

The code means that if this is the front page, we will display posts from the category **frontpage** only. So the first ten lines of this file will look like this:

```php
<?php get_header(); ?>
<?php get_sidebar(); ?>
```

```
<hr />
<div id="content">
<? if (is_home())
{
  query_posts("category_name='frontpage'");
}
?>
<?php if (have_posts()) : while (have_posts()) : the_post(); ?>
```

Save this file and refresh the front page of your blog. You will find that all the posts are gone except those categorized as **frontpage**.

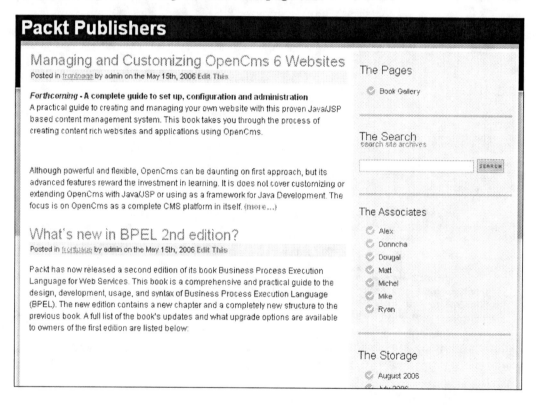

We are now seeing posts only from the **frontpage** category, which was a pretty easy task.

Step 4: Turn off Commenting on Front Page Posts

As it is a site for a publishing firm, we may not want to display public comments on the front page posts or allow commenting on the posts that we are displaying on the front page. Therefore, to turn off commenting for these posts, just open the posts for editing and turn off commenting by unchecking the checkbox **Allow Comments** from the right side, under the **Discussion** panel.

If you refresh the front page and click on any of the posts, you will find them displaying **Comments are closed**. However, the link **0 Comments** is still present on the front page. Now it's time to remove that link from the front page.

Open the index.php file using any editor and search for the following code block:

```
<div class="comments">
  <?php wp_link_pages(); ?>
  <?php comments_popup_link(__('<strong>0</strong> Comments'), __
('<strong>1</strong> Comment'), __('<strong>%</strong> Comments')); ?>
</div>
```

We need to tell WordPress that if it is the home page, then don't display the link. So add a small logic test before this code block and modify it like this:

```
<? if (single_cat_title("",false)!="frontpage"):?>
  <div class="comments">
    <?php wp_link_pages(); ?>
    <?php comments_popup_link(__('<strong>0</strong> Comments'), __
('<strong>1</strong> Comment'), __('<strong>%</strong> Comments')); ?>
  </div>
<? endif; ?>
```

The line single_cat_title("",false) returns the category name of the current post. So we simply checked that the current category is not **frontpage**; if not we still display the number of comments, using the function comments_popup_link; otherwise the link is skipped.

Packt Publishers

Managing and Customizing OpenCms 6 Websites

Posted in frontpage by admin on the May 15th, 2006

Forthcoming - A complete guide to set up, configuration and administration
A practical guide to creating and managing your own website with this proven Java/JSP based content management system. This book takes you through the process of creating content rich websites and applications using OpenCms. Although powerful and flexible, OpenCms can be daunting on first approach, but its advanced features reward the investment in learning. It is does not cover customizing or extending OpenCms with Java/JSP or using as a framework for Java Development. The focus is on OpenCms as a complete CMS platform in itself. (more...)

What's new in BPEL 2nd edition?

Posted in frontpage by admin on the May 15th, 2006

Packt has now released a second edition of its book Business Process Execution Language for Web Services. This book is a comprehensive and practical guide to the design, development, usage, and syntax of Business Process Execution Language (BPEL). The new edition contains a new chapter and a completely new structure to the previous book. A full list of the book's updates and what upgrade options are available to owners of the first edition are listed below:

The Pages

The Search
search site archives

[   ] SEARCH

The Associates

- Alex
- Donncha
- Dougal
- Matt
- Michel
- Mike
- Ryan

Step 5: Populate Some Data

Now it's time to add some data to our database. As our website is a general-purpose website for publishers, we must have some books. We have to categorize each book in different book categories. In our sample website, we have four categories. Before populating data, let's create these four categories from the administration panel. We will make every book entry as a regular post, but they must belong to appropriate categories.

- Open-source
- Java
- PHP
- Content Management System

Don't worry about the display of these posts. They will not appear in the front page, since we are displaying only some specific posts on our front page.

Step 6: Create Category Pages

Now we have to create some category pages. If our visitor clicks on any category, they will see just the titles of the books. When they click on the title of one of these books, they can see the details about that particular book.

So we have to modify our theme again. Let us open the `index.php` file inside our theme, i.e. in the **Green Marine** folder, and modify it as shown in the following code segment:

```
<?if (is_category()) $cat=true;?>
<?php get_header(); ?>
<?php get_sidebar(); ?>


<hr />
<div id="content">
<?php if (is_home())
{
   query_posts("category_name='frontpage'");
        $homepage= true;
}
?>
<?php if (have_posts()) : while (have_posts()) : the_post(); ?>

   <?php // Post dates off by default the_date('','<h2>','</h2>'); ?>
   <div id="post-<?php the_ID(); ?>">
   <h2><a href="<?php the_permalink() ?>" rel="bookmark">
   <?php the_title(); ?></a></h2>
<? if(!$cat):?>
   <div class="meta">
   <?php _e("Posted in"); ?> <?php the_category(',') ?>
   by <?php the_author() ?> on the <?php the_time('F jS, Y') ?>

   <?php edit_post_link(__('Edit This')); ?></div>
   <div class="main">
     <?php the_content(__('(more...)')); ?>
   </div>
<?endif;?>
   </div>

<? if (single_cat_title("",false)!="frontpage"):?>
<? if(!$cat):?>
<div class="comments">
    <?php wp_link_pages(); ?>
    <?php comments_popup_link(__('<strong>0</strong> Comments'), __
('<strong>1</strong> Comment'), __('<strong>%</strong> Comments')); ?>
  </div>
<? endif;?>
<? endif; ?>
<?php comments_template(); ?>
```

```
<?php endwhile; else: ?>
<div class="warning">
  <p><?php _e('Sorry, no posts matched your criteria, please try and
search again.'); ?></p>
</div>
<?php endif; ?>


<?php posts_nav_link(' &#8212; ', __('&laquo; Previous Page'), __
('Next Page &raquo;')); ?>


  </div>
<!-- End float clearing -->
</div>
<!-- End content -->
<?php get_footer(); ?>
```

If you look at the preceding code, you will find the modified code highlighted. At the top-most line, we just check whether the page is a category page. If so, we initialize a variable as `true`. We did this at the top of the page because the `is_category()` function always returns `true` inside a WordPress 'post' loop; so we must check it outside the loop. After that we skipped displaying the details of the post, if it is a category page. Finally, we hid the pop-up comment link. Now if you visit a particular category, you will see the following screen:

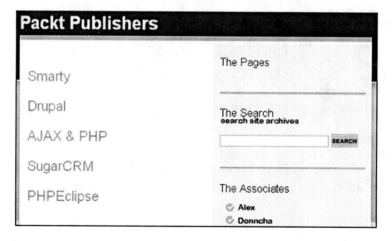

This is the typical look of a category where we display only the titles of the books. Each of these links is clickable and will navigate to the book's details when clicked.

You may not find the layout of the screen satisfactory. However, you can display it any way you want; you just have to know some CSS coding and that's all. You can do the rest. For the sake of simplicity, I skipped that part in this book.

Step 7: Add Some Description to Each Category Page

We will now add some description at the top of each category page. For example, when people click on the **Open-Source** category, they will see a detailed description of this category and what type of books are covered here. After that description, we will display our regular listing of books. Each category page must show its unique description. Let us take a look at the following screenshot:

Packt Publishers

Blah Blah Blah - Some description for category "OpenSource" Blah Blah Blah - Some description for category "OpenSource" Blah Blah Blah - Some description for category "OpenSource" Blah Blah Blah - Some description for category "OpenSource" Blah Blah Blah - Some description for category "OpenSource" Blah Blah Blah - Some description for category "OpenSource" Blah Blah Blah - Some description for category "OpenSource" Blah Blah Blah - Some description for category "OpenSource" Blah Blah Blah - Some description for category "OpenSource" Blah Blah Blah - Some description for category "OpenSource"

Mastering Mambo

Smarty

Drupal

SugarCRM

The preceding page is displayed when someone clicks on the **Open-Source** category. Let us take a look at another category page:

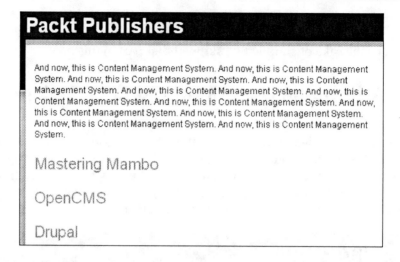

This is the **CMS** category. Please note that these two category pages each display their own description at the top of the page.

To achieve this functionality, we must add some description to each category from the administration panel. Let us log into the admin panel and select the **Manage** menu. Now click on the **Categories** sub-menu. You will find every category in your WordPress blog listed in this category management panel. Beside each category there is an **Edit** link. Click on that link and you will find the page where you can add a description for them.

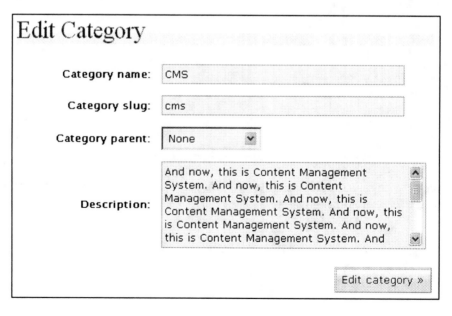

After adding some description, save it by clicking on the **Edit Category** button.

Now we have to modify our theme so that we can display these descriptions at the top of each category page. We first have to extract the description of the current category. Unfortunately, there is no built-in function in WordPress to do that. However, we can make use of some other functions. Firstly, we have to extract the current category name. We can do that using the `single_cat_title()` function. After that we must retrieve the current category object from which we can get the category description. Let's take a look at the code of the `index.php` file in our theme:

```
<?if (is_category()) $cat=true;?>
<?php  get_header(); ?>
<?php get_sidebar(); ?>

<hr />
<div id="content">
<?php if (is_home())
{
   query_posts("category_name='frontpage'");
         $homepage= true;
}
?>
<?
$catobj=get_category(get_cat_ID(single_cat_title('',false)));
echo $catobj->category_description;
?>
<?php if (have_posts()) : while (have_posts()) : the_post(); ?>

   <?php // Post dates off by default the_date('','<h2>','</h2>'); ?>
   <div id="post-<?php the_ID(); ?>">
   <h2><a href="<?php the_permalink() ?>" rel="bookmark">
   <?php the_title(); ?></a></h2>
<? if(!$cat):?>
   <div class="meta">
   <?php _e("Posted in"); ?> <?php the_category(',') ?> by
   <?php the_author() ?> on the <?php the_time('F jS, Y') ?>

   <?php edit_post_link(__('Edit This')); ?></div>
   <div class="main">
     <?php the_content(__('(more...)')); ?>
   </div>
<?endif;?>
   </div>

<? if (single_cat_title("",false)!="frontpage"):?>
```

```
<? if(!$cat):?>
<div class="comments">
    <?php wp_link_pages(); ?>
    <?php comments_popup_link(__('<strong>0</strong> Comments'), __
('<strong>1</strong> Comment'), __('<strong>%</strong> Comments')); ?>
  </div>
<? endif;?>
<? endif; ?>
<?php comments_template(); ?>

<?php endwhile; else: ?>
<div class="warning">
  <p><?php _e('Sorry, no posts matched your criteria, please try and
search again.'); ?>
  </p>
</div>
<?php endif; ?>

<?php posts_nav_link(' &#8212; ', __('&laquo; Previous Page'), __
('Next Page &raquo;')); ?>

  </div>
<!-- End float clearing -->
</div>
<!-- End content -->
<?php get_footer(); ?>
```

If you take a look at the preceding highlighted code, you will find that we used three functions, namely single_cat_title(), get_cat_ID(), and get_category(). The get_cat_id() function returns the ID of a category when the name of that category is supplied to this function as a parameter, and the get_category() function returns a category object when the category ID is passed as a parameter to it. When the following line of code executes, we get a category object in the $catObj variable:

```
$catobj=get_category(get_cat_ID(single_cat_title('',false)));
```

Now we will just access its description property and display it:

```
echo $catobj->category_description;
```

That's it! Notice how we can achieve some great functionality with just a few lines of code.

Step 8: An All Books Section

Well, now we need to display all the books in one single page despite their parent category. That is, whether a book belongs to the **Java** category or the **open-source** category, they must all show up in the **All Books** page.

We have to first create a category named **All Books** from the **Category** section. Then we can proceed further with the other tasks.

Next, we just have to modify all our book posts and add the category that we created earlier as **All Books**. That is, a book that belongs to the **PHP** category or whatever other category, must also belong to this **All Books** category.

For this, just log into the admin panel and then select the **Manage** menu. Create a category called **All Books** from the **Category** sub-menu. Now click on the **Posts** sub-menu and edit each post to add the **All Books** category to it from the right-hand side category pane. From now on, for every book that you will add, add a parent category under which that book should display and of course this **All Books** category.

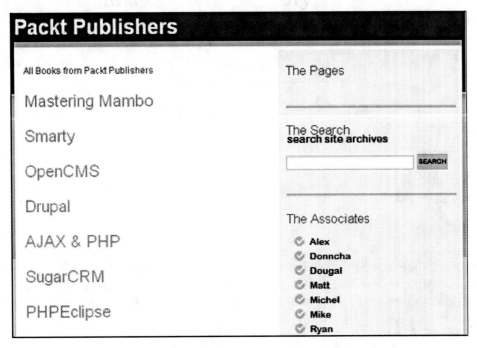

Now we have all our books displayed on one single page. Simple tricks save a lot of time. When you are not very familiar with the internals of WordPress, you may be scared to do a lot of coding for simple tasks. However, in real life WordPress is so flexible and extensible that you can do almost everything with this amazing blog engine.

Step 9: Customize the Categories

Now it's time to decorate our **Category** menu so that it shows only the necessary categories and no extra ones. If we look at our **Category** menu now, we will find all our categories being displayed and creating a total mess. Let us take a look:

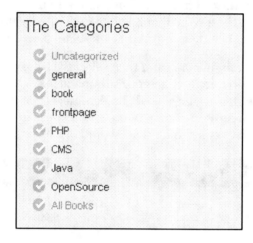

That's definitely not the look we want. We want to display only the following menus here:

- PHP
- CMS
- Open-Source
- Java
- All Books

We need to exclude all other unnecessary menus from the list. There are again some built-in features that we can make use of. Now we need to modify the sidebar.php file inside our theme. If you open the file, you will find that the following segment is responsible for displaying the categories in a list.

```php
<h3><?php _e('The Categories'); ?></h3>
<ul>
  <?php wp_list_cats(); ?>
</ul>
```

This `wp_list_cats()` function generates a list from all the available categories and returns them in a list. Now we want to exclude some of these categories from being displayed. The `Wp_list_cats()` function supports category exclusion. All we have to do is to supply the IDs of the categories that we want to hide as a parameter to this function. However, we need to know the category IDs for this.

Now log into the administration panel and choose the **Categories** sub-menu from **Manage**. You will find a page that looks like the following screenshot:

Categories (add new)

ID	Name	Description	# Posts	Action
12	All Books	All Books from Packt Publishers	7	Edit Delete
5	book		1	Edit Delete
9	CMS	And now, this is Content Management System. And now, this is Content Management System. And now, this is Content Management System. And now, this is Content Management System. And now, this is Content Management System. And now, this is Content Management System. And now, this is Content Management System. And now, this is Content Management System. And now, this is Content Management System. And now, this is Content Management System. And now, this is Content Management System.	3	Edit Delete
6	frontpage		7	Edit Delete
2	general		1	Edit Delete
10	Java		1	Edit Delete
		Blah Blah Blah – Some description for category "OpenSource" Blah Blah Blah – Some description for category "OpenSource" Blah Blah Blah – Some description for category "OpenSource" Blah Blah Blah – Some description for category		

Here, you find all the categories in our blog. In the left-most column, you will find their ID. In the preceding screenshot, we have noted the IDs we want to exclude. Those are **5, 6, 2,** and **1**. Now let us edit the `wp_list_cats()` function in `sidebar.php` as follows:

```
<h3><?php _e('The Categories'); ?></h3>
<ul>
  <?php wp_list_cats("exclude=2,5,1,6"); ?>
</ul>
```

Now refresh your WordPress blog and take a look at the category panel.

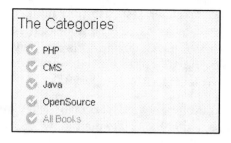

Now we have excluded all the unnecessary categories from our category panel. However, there is still something more to do. If you look at your category panel, you will find that the categories are displayed in no specific order. We can show them in ascending or descending order. For this we need to modify the preceding code block as shown below:

```
<h3><?php _e('The Categories'); ?></h3>
<ul>
  <?php wp_list_cats("exclude=2,5,1,6&sort_column=name"); ?>
</ul>
```

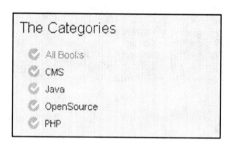

Now it is sorted and looks perfect. However, we don't want a title like **The Categories**. Let us make it **Book Categories**. Just modify the preceding code block and replace the The Categories text with Book Categories.

```
<h3><?php _e('Book Categories'); ?></h3>
<ul>
  <?php wp_list_cats("exclude=2,5,1,6&sort_column=name"); ?>
</ul>
```

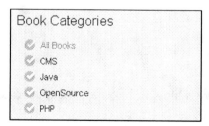

Now it perfectly fits with what we want.

Step 10: Adding the About Us Page and Author Page

Now we will add some other static pages as we planned earlier while planning the site structure. There will be a page about the company and a page solely for authors. Both of these pages are static and they will be displayed as a page, not regular posts. Besides these two static pages, we must have an image gallery and a top-ranked book list.

Let us add these static pages first. That will not be a big job at all. Just add them as pages, and you are done!

Step 11: Top Ranked Book List

This is a slightly tough part of this chapter. To display some books as top-listed books we have several options. We may create a manual list by editing the sidebar; however, it will not be dynamic at all and is not an acceptable solution. A better solution is to create a real top books list by counting the number of views of each book and dynamically displaying them. For this purpose, we need to create a plug-in on our own. Don't worry, we will keep it simple.

To make this plug-in work properly, we have to store the number of hits in persistent storage, that is where we can re-use them. You can use the database for storing them and that will be the best solution. However, as we are going for a simple plug-in, we will be using a simple text file for this purpose; but remember to use the database (either MySQL or SQLite) wherever possible. If you are already familiar with PHP coding, you can modify the code to suit any database table instead of a flat file.

Now we will design a plug-in, which adds a one pixel by one pixel image to the content of every post dynamically. The image will refer to a PHP file that will act as a hit counter after each call. The following code explains this:

```
<?
/*
Plugin Name: Hit Counter
Plugin URI: Uh.. No URL
Description: A plugin which counts the number of times a post been
viewed
Author: Hasin Hayder
Version: 1.0
Author URI: http://hasin.wordpress.com
*/
```

```
?>
<?
add_filter("the_content","HitCount");
function HitCount($content)

{

  global $id;

  $categories = get_the_category();
  foreach($categories as $category)
  {
    if ($category->cat_name=="All Books")
    return $content."<img style='display:none '
         src='http://wordpress_url/hitcount.php?id={$id}'>;
  }
  return $content;
?>
```

Please replace `wordpress_url` with your WordPress installation URL. Save this file as `hitcounter.plugin.php` and place this file in the `/wp-content/plugins` folder using any FTP client.

Now log into the admin panel and click on the **Plugin** menu. You will see a list of all the available plug-ins. The plug-in (**HitCounter**) also appears here. From this admin panel, you can activate and deactivate any plug-in. However, don't activate the **HitCounter** plug-in. We have something else to do.

Plugin Management

Plugins extend and expand the functionality of WordPress. Once a plugin is installed, you may activate it or deactivate it here.

Plugin	Version	Description	Action
Akismet	1.14	Akismet checks your comments against the Akismet web serivce to see if they look like spam or not. You need a WordPress.com API key to use this service. You can review the spam it catches under "Manage" and it automatically deletes old spam after 15 days. Hat tip: Michael Hampton and Chris J. Davis for help with the plugin. *By Matt Mullenweg.*	Activate
Hit Counter	1.0	A plugin which counts the number of times a post been viewed *By Hasin Hayder* .	Activate
Hello Dolly	1.5	This is not just a plugin, it symbolizes the hope and enthusiasm of an entire generation summed up in two words sung most famously by Louis Armstrong: Hello, Dolly. When activated you will randomly see a lyric from Hello, Dolly in the upper right of your admin screen on every page. *By Matt Mullenweg.*	Activate

Now we need to create another file called `hitcount.php` in the root directory of our WordPress installation.

```php
<?
$id = $_GET['id'];
$unserialized_data = file_get_contents("hits.txt");
  if (empty($unserialized_data))
  {
    $hits = array();
  }
  else
  {
    $hits = unserialize($unserialized_data);
  }
  //echo "<pre>".print_r($hits, true)."</pre>";
  $hits[$id]=$hits[$id]+1 ;
  $fp=fopen("hits.txt","w");
  flock($fp, LOCK_NB);
  fwrite($fp, serialize($hits));
  flock($fp,LOCK_UN);
  fclose($fp);
?>
```

We need to do one more thing. Let us create a file called `hits.txt` in your WordPress root directory using an FTP client and change its permission to `665` or rw-rw-r—.

Now we need to create a function that generates our top books list. Let us modify our `hitcounter.plugin.php` file as follows:

```php
<?
/*
Plugin Name: Hit Counter
Plugin URI: Uh.. No URL
Description: A plugin which counts the number of times a post been
viewed
Author: Hasin Hayder
Version: 1.0
Author URI: http://hasin.wordpress.com
*/
?>
<?
add_filter("the_content","HitCount");
function HitCount($content)
{
```

```
    global $id;
    $categories = get_the_category();
    foreach($categories as $category)
    {
      if ($category->cat_name=="All Books")
      return $content."<img style='display:none '
          src='http://localhost/wp/hitcount.php?id={$id}'>";
    }
    return $content;

  function GetTopBooks($limit=10)
  {
    $top_books = array();
    $unserialized_data = file_get_contents("hits.txt");
    $hits = @unserialize($unserialized_data);
    $limit=$limit>count($hits)?count($hits):$limit;
    $i=0;
    if (is_array($hits))
    {
    arsort($hits, SORT_DESC);

      foreach($hits as $post_id=>$post_hit)
      {
        $i++;
        if ($i>$limit) break;
        //$post_id = $hits[$i];
        $current_post = get_post($post_id);
        $top_books[] =
        "<li><a href='http://localhost/wp/?p={$post_id}'>".
        $current_post->post_title."<a/></li>";
      }
    }
    return implode($top_books);
  }
?>
```

Now we have a GetTopBooks() function that returns the list of top books in an array. We are going to use it in sidebar.php.

So modify sidebar.php as follows. The added portion of code has been highlighted.

```
<!-- begin sidebar -->
<div id="right">
  <!--
    <div id="author">
```

Here is a section you can use to briefly talk about yourself or
your site. Uncomment and delete this line to use.

```
        <h3><?php _e('The Author'); ?></h3>
        <p>Your description here.</p>
    </div>
    <div class="line"></div>
  -->
    <div id="links">

    <div id="pages">
      <h3><?php _e('The Pages'); ?></h3>
        <ul>
          <?php wp_list_pages('title_li='); ?>
        </ul>
    </div>

    <div class="line"></div>

    <h3>The Search</h3>
      <p class="searchinfo">search site archives</p>
      <div id="search">
        <div id="search_area">
          <form id="searchform" method="get" action=
            "<?php echo $_SERVER['PHP_SELF']; ?>">
            <input class="searchfield" type="text" name="s"
             id="s" value="" title="Enter keyword to search" />
            <input class="submit" type="submit" name=
            "submit" value="" title="Click to search archives" />
          </form>
        </div>
      </div>
    <div class="line"></div>
    <h3>Top Books</h3>
    <ul>
    <?=GetTopBooks()?>
    </ul>

    <div class="line"></div>

    <h3><?php _e('The Associates'); ?></h3>
      <ul>
        <?php get_links('-1', '<li>', '</li>', '', 0, 'name', 0, 0,
-1, 0); ?>
      </ul>
    <div class="line"></div>
```

```
    <h3><?php _e('The Storage'); ?></h3>
      <ul>
        <?php wp_get_archives('type=monthly'); ?>
      </ul>

<div class="line"></div>

      <h3><?php _e('Book Categories'); ?></h3>
        <ul>
          <?php wp_list_cats("exclude=2,5,1,6&sort_column=name"); ?>
        </ul>
<div class="line"></div>

      <h3><?php _e('The Meta'); ?></h3>
        <ul>
          <!-- <li><?php // wp_register(); ?></li> -->
          <li>Hello</li>
          <li><?php wp_loginout(); ?></li>
          <li><a href="http://wordpress.org/" title=
          "<?php _e('Powered by WordPress, state-of-the-art
                     semantic personal publishing platform.'); ?>">
           <abbr title="WordPress">WP</abbr>
          </a></li>
          <li><a href="http://gmpg.org/xfn/">
              <abbr title="XHTML Friends Network">XFN</abbr>
          </a></li>
          <li><a href="feed:<?php bloginfo('rss2_url'); ?>"
              title="<?php _e('Syndicate this site using RSS'); ?>">
           <?php _e('<abbr title="Really Simple Syndication">
              RSS</abbr>'); ?>
          </a></li>
          <li><a href="feed:<?php bloginfo('comments_rss2_url'); ?>"
              title="<?php _e('The latest comments to all posts
              in RSS'); ?>">
        <?php _e('Comments <abbr title="Really Simple
              Syndication">RSS</abbr>'); ?>
          </a></li>
          <li><a href="#content" title="back to top">Back to top
          </a></li>
          <?php wp_meta(); ?>
        </ul>

    </div>

</div>
<!-- end sidebar -->
```

This will add the top books list in the sidebar as follows:

As soon as any visitor visits any book, the data will be updated and the list will be sorted accordingly.

Step 12: Adding Links of Associates

Now it's time to add some links of our associates. The associates will be displayed under a special **Associates** section. To add a link in our WordPress installation, log into the admin panel and select **Links**. You will see the available list of links as shown in the following screenshot:

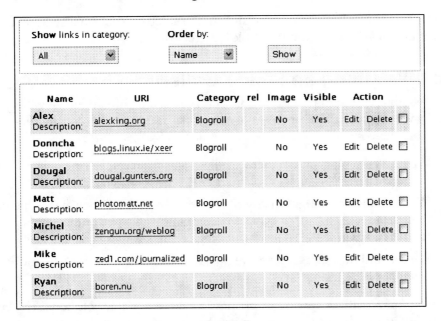

You can manage all existing links from here. However, to add a new link just select the **Add Link** sub-menu under this menu. You will be redirected to a page where you can add new links.

| Manage Links | **Add Link** | Link Categories | Import Links |

Add a link:

Basics

URI:

Link Name:

Short description:

Category: 1 : Blogroll

Add Link »

As soon as you add a link, it will be visible in the sidebar. You can also add links under different categories from the **Link Categories** menu.

Step 13: Adding an Image Gallery

Now here's another tough part of our project. We need to add an image gallery where we will display all cover pages of our books as images. To do this, let us see our possible choices:

- We can use a plug-in that extracts all images from a specific directory and displays them.

- We can store our images in any photo organizer (like Flickr) and displaying them from that organizer using any compatible plug-in; but we are not going to do that when we are deploy our blog in our self-managed hosting.

- We can add images as a separate post that will link to each of the individual original posts.

In this section, we will see how to implement all these possible solutions. The best solution for our problem is the third option. However, in different scenarios the other two options would be considered as the best solution. So let's start one by one.

Solution 1: Extract Images from a Specific Directory

For this, we need to design a plug-in that extracts all images from any specific directory and displays them as a gallery. Moreover, when someone clicks on any of those images, it will redirect to its corresponding book post. To accomplish this, we need to follow one rule, and that is, we must name each image according to the format `PostId-imagetitle.ImageExtension`.

Let us now design the plug-in. It will extract all images from the **coverpage** folder inside our WordPress root directory.

```php
<?
/*
Plugin Name: Image Gallery
Plugin URI: Uh.. No URL
Description: A plugin which displays all images under any dir as image
gallery
Author: Hasin Hayder
Version: 1.0
Author URI: http://hasin.wordpress.com
*/
?>
<?
add_filter("the_content", "ImageGallery");

function ImageGallery($content)
{
  if (strpos($content, "{gallery}")!==false)
  {
    $content = str_replace("{gallery}","",$content );
    $fp = opendir("coverpage");
    $table = "<table cellpadding='5' cellspacing='5'>";
    $i=false;
    while ($dir = readdir($fp)) {
      if (is_file("coverpage/{$dir}"))
      {
        if(false==$i)
        {
          $table .="<tr>";
        }
        $i = !$i;
        $file = split("-",$dir);
        $post_id = $file[0];

        $table .="<td>
```

```
            <a href='http://localhost/wp/?p={$post_id}'>
            <img src=''http://localhost/wp/coverpage/{$dir}'></a></td>";
            if(false==$i)
            {
               $table .="</tr>";
            }
         }
      }
      $table .= "</table>";
   }
   return $content.$table;
}
?>
```

Now save this file as `imagegallery.plugin.php` in the `wp-contents/plugin` folder. Next enable the plug-in from the **Plugin** administration panel.

To see the plug-in in action, create a folder named **coverpage** in the WordPress root directory. Inside the directory, place some image following the exact naming convention `postid-filename.extension`.

Now let us create a new page where you just add the string {**gallery**}. Please note that it is a page and not a regular post, since we are displaying this gallery as a separate page in our blog. You can also add some additional text; but {**gallery**} must be present in the content of the text.

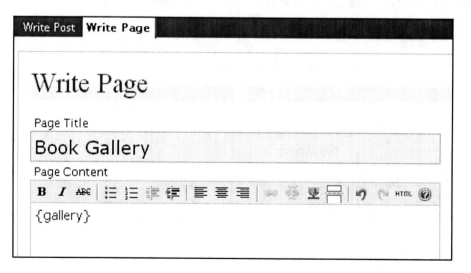

That is all! Visit this page in your browser, and you will see the image gallery.

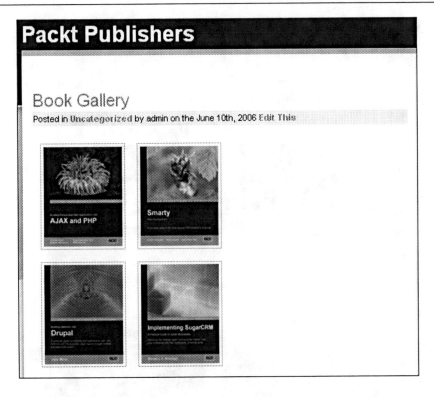

Please note that you must add the string {gallery} wherever you want to display this image gallery. The string {gallery} can be added to any post or any page. Whenever you add the text {gallery} in the content, it will display the gallery there. It is not specific to this page only.

Solution 2: Image from Photo Organizer

There are some interesting plug-ins already available for this purpose. FAlbum does its job pretty well, if you are using photos from your existing Flickr account. If you are using any other popular image organizer/gallery script like Gallery or Coppermine, please take a look at the Codex plug-in directory for appropriate plug-ins.

Solution 3: Creating a Gallery Manually

This is the easiest step among these three solutions. Here all we need to do is to create a page where we add every image using the `<img>` tag or simply using the built-in image browser button at the bottom of the **Write Page**. Before that, we need to upload each and every book image with the built-in uploader of WordPress. Next, we will add those pictures one by one manually to our page. We can also add hyperlinks to these images using the `<a>` tag or by clicking the link button from the toolbar. That's it. Take a look at the following screenshot:

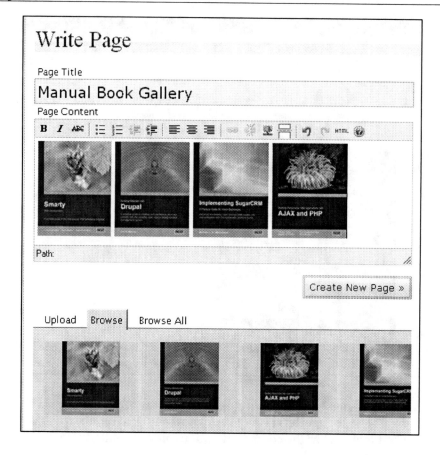

Summary

In this chapter, we have learned how to create a complete general-purpose website with WordPress. These posts are considered as non-blog content. WordPress provides an extremely flexible set of APIs with which you can extend your theme and achieve almost every kind of functionality with minimum effort and code modification.

If you study the WordPress API from Codex, you will learn how to extend WordPress in more depth than discussed here. Moreover, we have two complete chapters on how to develop themes and plug-ins from scratch. In those chapters, we will discuss WordPress APIs in more details. For now, please review the modifications that you have just done in this chapter and try to play with them by modifying them according to your requirements.

6
Feeds and Podcasting

In this chapter, we will introduce you to the new buzzword in the Internet content management world. Since its invention in 1990, the World Wide Web has become the biggest repository of information. The total amount of information stored in servers located in different places on earth is tremendous and we can't even imagine it! With this ample information, it is really difficult to find out what is necessary for us. The evolution of search engines like Yahoo, Google, and Lycos make it a bit easier to locate the information. However, it's really a big job to deliver content to your readers and to read the necessary data. To keep yourself up to date with this vast amount of information you need an easy way to proceed.

Feeds were developed to address this problem. RSS feeds basically provide information about a web-based resource, its URL, its title, a short description, and sometimes links to other documents that are relevant to it. In this chapter, we will discuss how feeds can change the concept of content delivery, content aggregation, and how to stay up-to-date using feeds. Feeds are now so developed that you can deliver almost any type of content with them.

What are Feeds All About?

A few years ago you used to receive up-to-date news in your mailbox. You couldn't avoid reading those big emails for valuable news. However, these mails were stored in the mailbox in such an unstructured and haphazard manner that tracing them for later use was really a big job. Most of the time, those mails were considered as one-time reading. Moreover, searching through mailboxes is sometimes not flexible and private business mailboxes are usually not big enough to store these big newsletters.

Yet another way of keeping yourself up to date is just visiting the website and checking manually if there is anything recent. However, there is no guarantee that you didn't overlook any item. In this process, you have to check the whole site to find out what's new.

Here comes the magic of feeds. Feeds are a short summary of content presented in a pre-defined structured way that tells you exactly what is new and up to date. Using feed aggregators (software that can read feeds), you can always stay up to date. You can even listen to podcasts using your feed aggregator. If you know what is new, you will not bother to do a manual search for information. Feeds were invented to deliver recent news to visitors and to avoid the boredom of searching for information.

History of Feeds

Whether it is the discovery of Newton's laws or Einstein's universal energy formula, there are always some great stories behind every innovation. To figure out how the RSS feeds evolved into the current state, let us take a look at their history. For starters, RSS stands for Really Simple Syndication.

Dave Winer of UserLand (http://www.userland.com) is the man mostly responsible for the evolution of RSS, the leading format for feeds. First he developed a system to deliver news, which he called scriptingNews. Thereafter, Dan Libby modified Winer's work to grab news and display it on the Netscape website. This time they only displayed a title, a link, and a small description. Due to this modification, Netscape users were able to read news aggregated from different sources into the Netscape website. If they were interested to read further, they could go directly to the original news source through the link provided.

Dan Libby's work was in some ways the first version of RSS. The process was called RDF, which stands for Resource Description Format. Using this format, anyone could publish the title, description, and link of any web-based resource. Shortly after Libby's work on RSS 0.9, he decided to bring about some major structural changes. The changed format was designated RSS 0.91.

In 2000, a group of developers created RSS 1.0 based on RDF. This version of RSS was a bit complicated with several modules. Developers could now use RSS to describe any resource. This version was a feature-rich pack of the original RSS. In the meantime, Dave Winer released the new edition of RSS 0.91, which he versioned as 0.92. At this time Netscape's original site, for which the RSS was developed, was shut down. However, many people had already started using RSS and they preferred to stay with the simple version of RSS, which was 0.91, and thus this version became the de facto.

In 2002, a new era began with the release of RSS 2.0. Dave Winer had left UserLand, but he was still interested in developing RSS formats. So he delivered this new version with some new features like publication date, a unique identifier, and support for namespaces.

In 2003, UserLand shifted the copyright of RSS 2.0 to Harvard while Dave Winer went to study for a year in Berkman Center for Internet and Society in Harvard.

During this time, an advisory committee for the evolution of RSS was formed. Meanwhile, based on some propositions on existing RSS formats by Sam Ruby, a developer in IBM, another feed format was born. The format was first called Echo, then Pie, and finally called Atom.

Some versions of RSS are based on RDF, while some are not. RSS 0.9 and 1.0 are based on original RDF. The modern RSS news aggregators can read all these formats. So you need not worry about which format to use to deliver content. However, the simplest RSS format is 0.91, which is better for faster delivery of your content. If you really don't want to deliver extended contents like images, audio, and video, then use the 0.91 version; otherwise, stay with RSS 2.0.

RSS Formats

We have gone through the history and evolution of the various RSS formats. In this section, we will take a short look at the structure of the different popular formats of RSS, especially 0.91, 1.0, and 2.0 and we will also take a look at Atom.

RSS 0.91

In RSS 0.91, everything is described under a channel. In a channel, there are several items. Every item has its own title, description, and link. A channel also features a title, link, and description of the whole RSS content. The following code block shows the typical format of RSS 0.91:

```
<?xml version="1.0"?>
<rss version="0.91">
<channel>
<title>the title of this feed</title>
<link>a valid URL to this feed</link>
<description>description of this feed</description>
<language>language code, for example en-us</language>
<item>
<title>Title of first item</title>
<link>Url of first item</link>
<description>Short description about this item.</description>
</item>
<item>
<title>Title of second item</title>
<link>Url of second item</link>
<description>Short description about this item.</description>
</item>
</channel>
</rss>
```

RSS 1.0

The following code block displays the typical format of RSS 1.0:

```
<?xml version="1.0"?>
<rdf:RDF
xmlns:rdf="http://www.w3.org/1999/02/22-rdf-syntax-ns#"
xmlns="http://purl.org/rss/1.0/"
xmlns:dc="http://purl.org/dc/elements/1.1/">
<channel rdf:about="http://www. put_website_url_here.com">
<title>The Name of the Feed</title>
<link>http://www. put_website_url_here.com</link>
<description>Feed description.</description>
<language>en-us</language>
<items>
<rdf:Seq>
<rdf:li rdf:resource="http://www.
put_website_url_here.com/page1.html" />
<rdf:li rdf:resource="http://www.
put_website_url_here.com/page2.html" />
</rdf:Seq>
</items>
</channel>
<item rdf:about="http://www.
put_website_url_here.com/page1.html">
<title>Title of First Item</title>
<link>http://www. put_website_url_here.com</link>
<description>The item 1 content.</description>
<dc:creator>Author</dc:creator>
<dc:date>yyyy-mm-dd</dc:date>
</item>
<item rdf:about="http://www.yoursite.com/page2.html">
<title>Title of Second Item</title>
<link>http://www. put_website_url_here.com</link>
<description>The item 2 content.</description>
<dc:creator>Author</dc:creator>
<dc:date>yyyy-mm-dd</dc:date>
</item>
</rdf:RDF>
```

RSS 2.0

Similar to the previous code blocks, the following code block displays the format for RSS 2.0:

```
<rss version="2.0">
<channel>
<title>The Name of the Feed</title>
<link>http://www. put_website_url_here.com</link>
<description>Feed Description.</description>
<language>en-us</language>
<copyright>Copyright notice</copyright>
<pubDate>Tue, 28 Nov 2006 11:02:03 GMT</pubDate>
<lastBuildDate>Tue, 5 Dec 2006 10:40:01 GMT</lastBuildDate>
<managingEditor>you@domain.com</managingEditor>
<webMaster>webmaster@domain.com</webMaster>
<item>
<title>Title of First Item</title>
<link>http://www.put_website_url_here.com</link>
<description>The item 1 content.</description>
<author>you@domain.com</author>
<pubDate>Tue, 28 Nov 2006 11:02:03 GMT</pubDate>
<enclosure url="http://www. put_website_url_here.com/
filename.mp3" length="0001" type="audio/mpeg"/>
<guid isPermaLink="false">id_01</guid>
</item>
<item>
<title>Title of Second Item</title>
<link>http://www. put_website_url_here.com</link>
<description>The item 2 content.</description>
<author>You@domain.com</author>
<pubDate>Tue, 28 Nov 2004 11:02:03 GMT</pubDate>
<enclosure url="http://www. put_website_url_here.com/
filename.mp3" length="0001" type="audio/mpeg"/>
<guid isPermaLink="false">id_02</guid>
</item>
</channel>
</rss>
```

Atom

The following code block shows the structure of Atom:

```
<?xml version="1.0" encoding="utf-8"?>
<feed xmlns="http://www.w3.org/2005/Atom">

  <title>Story title</title>
  <subtitle>Story sub Title</subtitle>
  <link href="http://packtpub.com/"/>
  <updated>2006-10-30T18:30:02Z</updated>
  <author>
```

```
  <name>Author</name>
  <email>email address</email>
</author>
<id>urn:uuid:60a76c80-d399-11d9-b91C-0003939e0af6</id>
<entry>
  <title>Wordpress Complete</title>
  <link href="http://packtpub.com/wordpress/book"/>
  <id>urn:uuid:1225c695-cfb8-4ebb-aaaa-80da344efa6a</id>
  <updated>2006-10-30T18:30:02Z</updated>
  <summary>WordPress is a fanastic CMS. This book covers everything
about WordPress.</summary>
  </entry>

</feed>
```

Feed Readers

After learning about feeds, you may wonder how these feeds are used or consumed by people in real life. Well, there are both web-based feed aggregators and desktop applications, which are called feed readers. These feed readers read feeds at a regular interval and mark the new items in bold (or with some other format). Thus, you can clearly understand what is new after your last visit to the particular website that produced the feed.

Some of the most popular feed readers are mentioned in the following list:

- RSS Owl: This is an incredibly small application built on Java SWT technology. It is fast, small, and easy to use. RSS Owl requires Java runtime to work properly. This is an open-source software that you can obtain from `http://www.rssowl.org`.

- Built-in feed reader of Firefox: The Firefox browser comes with a built-in feed reader. So whenever you point your browser to a feed URL, it is displayed in a nice and pleasing readable format.

- Google feed reader: Google feed reader is another popular feed-reading tool. You can manage your feeds by keeping track of them and the Google reader will nicely display the feeds that have updated information.

Producing Feeds

You may wonder how these feeds are generated, especially in our WordPress blogs. Well, the whole process is automated. The WordPress distribution pack comes with a feed generator. The feed generator generates feeds from posts, comments, and even categories. The WordPress feed generator generates both Atom and RSS feeds.

You can find the feed generator in the WordPress blog if you point your browser to any of the following URLs: `http://your_wordpress_installation_path/wp-rss.php`, `http://your_wordpress_installation_path/wp-rss2.php`, `http://your_wordpress_installation_path/wp-commentsrss2.php`, and `http://your_wordpress_installation_path/wp-atom.php`. Let's take a look at the following screenshot that we can see when we browse to the `wp-rss.php` URL:

Packt Publishers

Just another WordPress weblog

Mastering Mambo

Mastering Mambo is a professional-level guide to Mambo's most powerful and useful features. You will develop powerful interactive sites that fit perfectly with your unique requirements. Create attractive custom layouts for Mambo. Build multilingual, Internationalised sites. Open an online store for your Mambo site, complete with support for gift coupons, ...

Smarty

This book is a comprehensive guide to all aspects of using Smarty. It will help you to: Install and configure Smarty on your Web server Understand how Smarty affects your web site architecture, and build site foundations that make the most of what Smarty offers ...

OpenCMS

This book takes you through the process of creating content-rich websites and applications using OpenCms. Although powerful and flexible, OpenCms can be daunting on first approach, but its advanced features reward the investment in learning. This book exists to ease Java developers into getting the most from OpenCms. With hard-won ...

This is the default look of our WordPress blog that we created in the previous chapter. The feeds are shown in a nice format using the built-in feed reader of Firefox (included in the Bon Echo version). Let us take a look at the raw source that generates it. To view the source, click on the **View** menu and select **Page Source**, or simply hit *Ctrl +u*.

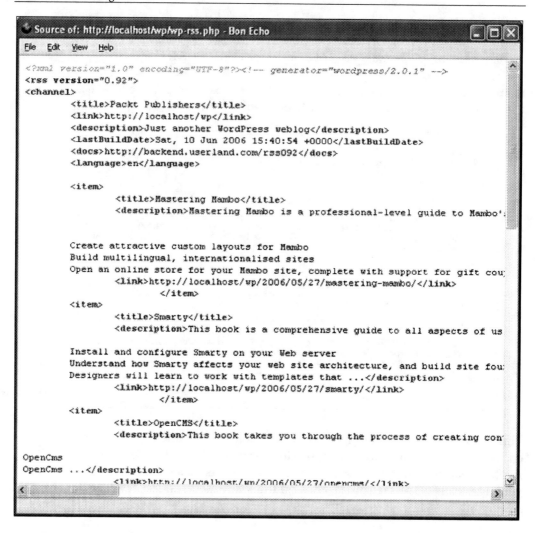

So you see that the `wp-rss.php` URL generates RSS 0.92 compliant feeds. If you browse `wp-rss2.php`, you will find that the sources are RSS 2.0-compliant.

So that's it. WordPress has built-in feed producers. If you want to provide an RSS links for posts in your blog, just point them to `wp-rss.php` and `wp-rss2.php`. For RSS feeds for comments, point to `wp-commentsrss.php`. For categories, point to `wp-rss.php` or `wp-rss2.php` along with a category ID. For example, `wp-rss.php?cat=15`; here, `15` is the category ID.

Consuming Feeds

In the *Feed Readers* section, we discussed how you can consume feeds using different desktop software. In this section, we will see how we can consume feeds from remote sources into your WordPress blog.

Whenever you need to consume and display feeds from another source, there will probably be one of two scenarios:

- First and most of the time, you want to consume feeds and display their content (mostly, just the title) in your sidebar.

- You may also consume feeds and display the title and a short description about it in your posts or pages. These posts will automatically display the latest feed contents whenever some visitor sees them.

In this section, we will discuss both cases and how to accomplish these tasks with our regular WordPress installation. In both these cases, we should use plug-ins. Sometimes we can use existing plug-ins, sometimes we can develop our own.

Feeds come in XML format. So if you want to fetch feed contents from a remote source, you will fetch an XML document that you need to parse and extract to display it in whatever format you want. In PHP, there are built-in XML parsers that can parse an XML document and supply you the contents in a usable way; for example, in arrays. However, to parse the XML document of an RSS feed, we are not going to re-invent the wheel by parsing it totally from scratch. There are several libraries to do the job for us; we only need to perform the rest of the job, which is to display the parsed content in a proper way. These libraries are open source, freely available under different open-source licenses like GPL, CC, and LGPL. A few of those that are most commonly used are lastRSS, magpieRSS, and SimplePie. Among these, I have found lastRSS to be very flexible to use.

Let's develop a small plug-in that displays content from an RSS feed inside a post or on a page. Firstly, let us create a PHP file named `rss.plugin.php` and save it in the `wp-content/plugin` folder. However, before that please download the `lastRSS.php` file from `lastrss.webdot.cz` (http://lastrss.webdot.cz/lastRSS.zip) and place it in the same folder. The `lastRSS.php` file contains RSS parsing functions, which are used by this plug-in. Here is the code for the plug-in:

```
<?
/*
Plug-in Name: RSS Processor
Plug-in URI: http://hasin.phpxperts.com/
Description: A plug-in that aggregates RSS and parses to show it, you
can use it in any post of any page
Author: Hasin Hayder
Version: 2.0
Author URI: http://hasin.phpxperts.com

Feature: now supports multi rss source in single post or page.
*/
?>
```

```
<?
include_once("./wp-content/plugins/lastRSS.php");
add_filter('the_content', 'rss_parse');

/**
rss_parse
this function searches the content for {rss} tag and then parses it

sample formats of the {rss} tag
  1. {rss uri=http://rss.groups.yahoo.com/group/phpexperts/rss
count=5}
  2. {rss uri=http://hasin.wordpress.com/wp-rss2.php count=10}

there are 2 attributes in this {rss} tag that we look for
  1. uri = rss feed location
  2. counter = how many feeds to show

@param string $content the content of the post
@return none
*/
function rss_parse($content)
{
  $rss = new lastRSS();

  $pattern = "~{rss\s*uri=(.*)\s*count=(.*)}~iU";

  preg_match_all($pattern, $content, $matches);
  $rsses =0;
  while ($rsses<count($matches[0]))
  {
    //initialize the content buffer
    $p_content = "";
    //get the rss uri
    $uri = $matches[1][$rsses];
    //get how many rss feed to show on page
    $count = $matches[2][$rsses];

    //initialize the counter
    if (empty($count)) $count = 10;

    //parse it
    $rss_content = $rss->Get($uri);
    //get all the items
    $items = $rss_content['items'];

    //parse the items
    $i=0;
    while($i<$count)
```

```php
        {
            $p_content .= "<div id='rss_item'><strong><a href='{$items[$i]['
link']}'>".$items[$i]['title']."</a></strong><br/>";
            $p_content .= "".$items[$i]['description']."</div><br/><br/>";

            $i++;

        }

        $content = str_replace($matches[0][$rsses], $p_content, $content);
        $rsses +=1;
    }
    return $content;
}

function rss_sidebar($rss_uri, $count)
{
    $rss = new lastRSS();
    $rss_content = $rss->Get($rss_uri);
    //get all the items
    $items = $rss_content['items'];

    //parse the items
    $i=0;
    echo "<ul>";
    while($i<$count)
    {
        echo "<li>"."<a href='".$items[$i]['link']."'>".$items[$i]['title'
]."</a></li>";
        $i++;
    }
    echo "</ul>";
}
?>
```

After finishing your code, activate the plug-in from your plug-in administration panel. You will find the plug-in as **RSS Processor**.

To see the plug-in in action, just add the following line to any post or page content:

```
{rss uri='http://some_feed_url' count=10}
```

Now, take a look at the following screenshot:

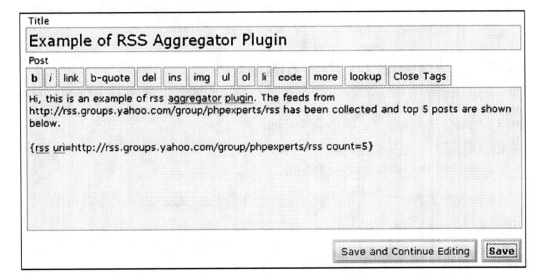

Now if you locate this post in the browser, you will find the following output:

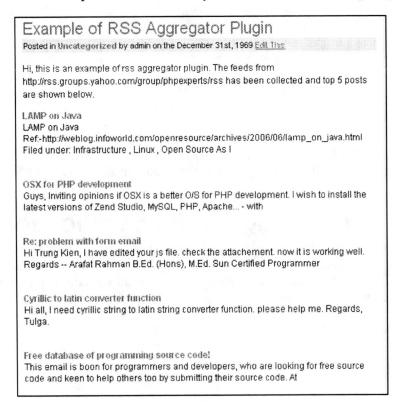

Please compare it with our post body. After the content that we type in our post, all the contents are dynamically extracted from the RSS feed URL and the top five posts are displayed.

Adding Feeds in the Sidebar

The `rss_sidebar()` function in this plug-in has been designed to display extracted feed titles in your sidebar. Open your sidebar file using the theme editor or any FTP client, and add the following code at the bottom:

```
<div class="line"></div>
<h3>Feeds from PHPExperts</h3>
<?
rss_sidebar("http://rss.groups.yahoo.com/group/phpexperts/rss",5);
?>
```

Now save the changes and open your blog in the browser. If you take a look at the bottom of your sidebar, you will find the feeds.

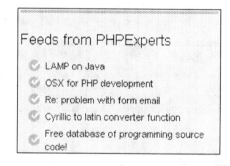

Thus, you can get whatever you want with minimal amount of coding. That's the magic of WordPress and that's why WordPress is so popular and extensible.

Other Useful Plug-ins for Syndication

There are several other very popular plug-ins for syndication in WordPress. Some help to fetch the feed contents from remote sources and display them in a more stylish way, some collect the latest posts from remote sources and display them turning your blog into a **planet**.

If you are involved with different developer communities, then you must be already familiar with **planets**. A planet is a kind of news aggregator that collects content from different blogs having the same interest. Usually, these planet applications collect news from RSS feeds of very popular and renowned blogs and display their contents in a single page. So if you browse a planet, you will instantly know what is hot and happening in the community. You will find some very popular planets like Planet-PHP (`http://planet-php.org`), Planet-MySQL (`http://www.planetmysql.org/`), Planet-Ruby (`http://planetruby.0x42.net/`), Planet-PostgreSQL (`http://www.planetpostgresql.org/`), and so forth.

You will find a list of available plug-ins at the following URL:

`http://codex.wordpress.org/Plugins/Syndication`

There are a number of plug-ins listed there, but the **FeedWordPress** plug-in is extremely useful, especially if you want to turn your WordPress blog into a planet.

FeedWordPress

FeedWordPress is a great plug-in if you want to aggregate posts from different blogs and display their content at a single place. In this section, we will discuss how to turn your blog into a planet using this great plug-in. FeedWordPress is developed by Charles Johnson (`http://radgeek.com/contact`) and you can download it from `http://projects.radgeek.com/feedwordpress/`.

Installing FeedWordPress is simple. After downloading and extracting the archive, you will find a folder named **wp-content** folder. Inside this folder, there are two files, namely `update-feeds.php` and `feedwordpress.php`. Place these files inside your WordPress directory as per the following directions:

1. Place `feedwordpress.php` inside your **plugins** folder (`wp-content/plugins/`).

2. Place `update-feeds.php` inside the **wp-content** folder.

Now go to your **Plugins** administration panel and activate this plug-in. You will find the plug-in as **Feed Wordpress**. After activating this plug-in, you will find an additional sub-menu **Syndication** under the **Options** menu. Take a look at the following screenshot:

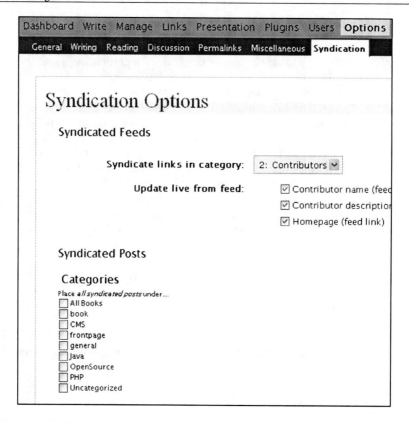

From this panel, you can syndicate remote feed contents under any specific category; you can also choose which items to syndicate.

If you scroll down the page, you will find a section with further more options:

Publication:	⦿ Publish syndicated posts immediately
	○ Hold syndicated posts as drafts
	○ Hold syndicated posts as private posts
Comments:	○ Allow comments on syndicated posts
	⦿ Don't allow comments on syndicated posts
Trackback and Pingback:	○ Accept pings on syndicated posts
	⦿ Don't accept pings on syndicated posts
Unfamiliar authors:	⦿ create a new author account
	○ attribute the post to the default author
	○ don't syndicate the post
Unfamiliar categories:	⦿ create any categories the post is in
	○ don't create new categories
	○ don't create new categories and don't syndicate posts unless they match at least one familiar category
Permalinks point to:	original website ▾

These settings provide more control over fetched contents, for example you can publish these feeds right after aggregating or you can hold them for moderation.

Podcasting

Podcasting is a way of sharing your blog in an audio format, which means you just record your voice on some topic and distribute it from your blog. Podcasters usually distribute content in RSS format or in Atom format. Podcast clients like iTune, Juice, and CastPodder are able to extract the content from your RSS feeds, download it into an audio player, and help the listeners listen to those files.

You may wonder how the podcast clients understand the music files as podcast. Well, whenever you make a post in your blog, a link to that post is automatically included in your blog RSS. While generating those RSS feeds, WordPress is intelligent enough to add an `<enclosure>` tag (available in RSS 2.0) if any music file is linked within that post. It will look something as follows in your blog RSS:

```
<enclosure url="http://your_domain/file_name.file_extension"
length="file_size_in_bytes" type="mime_type_of_this_file" />
```

Please note that the `<enclosure>` tag is a sub-tag of the `<item>` tag. So your job is to make a post and WordPress will do the rest for you. However, there are certain issues; let us now have a detailed look at podcasting.

How to Podcast

For basic podcasting, just follow the directions given as follows:

Record your voice: You can record your voice or whatever you want to podcast using any commercial or free software and save it as an MP3 file. There are several commercial applications for working with sound; however, if you want to go for free software, I would recommend **Audacity**. This is a cross-platform sound editor. You can download Audacity from the following URL: `http://audacity.sourceforge.net/`. There is a free applications that runs on Windows and works pretty fine; it is called **WavePad**. You can download WavePad from `http://www.nch.com.au/wavepad/`.

Upload to a server: You can now upload your recorded music files onto your server or anywhere you want. You can also use `archive.org` to upload free of cost to host your audio files free of cost. However, there are some issues; if you use `archive.org`, you will find that it gives you a URL that actually redirects to the music content behind the scene. Now, when you make a post that links to your `archive.org` music file, WordPress can't detect the redirection and hence it can't add the music file in the `<enclosure>` tag. To solve this issue, Tom Raftery's blog (`http://www.tomrafteryit.net/wordpress-podcasts-not-showing-up-fixed/`) has a solution where he recommends doing the following; and it works.

- While creating a post, scroll down to the bottom section and you will find a section named **Add custom field**. Just add a key named **enclosure** and type the URL of your music file as the value of that key.

- For subsequent posts, just select the item **key** from the custom field key drop-down box, and type the URL of the music file as its value.

Make a post: After successfully uploading to any server, now its time to make a post. Please be careful, you must add a link to the absolute URL (that means the exact URL pointing to that audio file) of the music file inside your post content. No relative content will work. Take a look at the following screenshot:

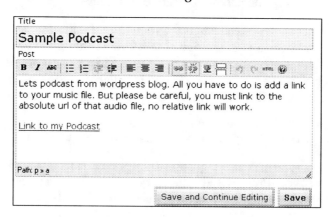

After saving this post, if you take a look at your RSS feed, you will find the first item (the post that you just made becomes your top item in RSS feeds) looking like this:

```
<item>
    <title>Sample Podcast</title>
    <link>http://localhost/wp/2006/06/27/sample-podcast/</link>
    <comments>http://localhost/wp/2006/06/27/sample-podcast/
#comments</comments>
    <pubDate>Tue, 27 Jun 2006 16:15:27 +0000</pubDate>
    <dc:creator>admin</dc:creator>

  <category>frontpage</category>
    <guid isPermaLink="false">
        http://localhost/wp/2006/06/27/sample-podcast/
    </guid>
    <description><![CDATA[Lets podcast from wordpress blog. All you
have to do is add a link to your music file. But please be careful,
you must link to the absolute url of that audio file, no relative link
will work.
Link to my Podcast

]]>
    </description>
    <content:encoded>
<![CDATA[<p>Lets podcast from wordpress blog. All you have to do is
add a link to your music file. But please be careful, you must link to
the absolute url of that audio file, no relative link will work.</p>
<p><a title="My Podcast" href="http://localhost/wp/my-podcast.
mp3">Link to my Podcast</a>
</p>
]]>
    </content:encoded>
    <wfw:commentRSS>
        http://localhost/wp/2006/06/27/sample-podcast/feed/
        </wfw:commentRSS>
        <enclosure url='http://localhost/wp/my-podcast.mp3'
                   length='1754254'
                   type='audio/mpeg'/>
</item>
```

Please notice the `<enclosure>` tag in the preceding feed entry. WordPress automatically detects the size of that audio file. So when someone subscribes to your blog RSS using iTune or any podcast client, this content will be automatically downloaded to his/her audio player for listening to that podcast.

Useful Plug-ins for Podcasting

There are plug-ins available for podcasting with WordPress. You can check the following two plug-ins for working further on podcasting:

Podpress (`http://www.mightyseek.com/podpress`) is a cool plug-in that will help you to podcast more smartly. This plug-in has built-in player support, preview support , video podcasting, and much more.

iPodCatter (`http://garrickvanburen.com/wordpress-plugins/wpipodcatter`) helps podcasters running WordPress to create a valid feed for iTunes' podcast directory and specify the `itunes:duration` and `itunes:explicit` tags on a per-episode basis.

Dedicated Podcasting

If you want a separate RSS feed just for your podcasts, then it is considered as dedicated podcasting. For this, you need to create a category like **my_podcasts** or something meaningful. Now whenever you make a podcast, just post under this special category **my_podcasts**.

We know that by default WordPress RSS contains all posts in its feed collection. However, to make a separate RSS feed URL just for this category, we need to browse the feed URL in the following format:

```
http://your_wordpress_installation/?feed=rss2&category_name=my_podcasts
```

If you browse this URL, you will find only the latest feeds from the **my_podcasts** category.

Summary

Feeds are a very important component for delivering the content of your blog to your readers. In this chapter, we learned what an RSS feed is and how to incorporate feeds within our WordPress blog. Though different versions of RSS are available, version 0.91 is the simplest while version 2.0 is feature-rich. If you want to deliver binary contents or audio/video files through your RSS, you must deliver the feeds in RSS 2.0 format.

In the next chapter, you will learn how to develop WordPress themes.

7
Developing Themes

One of the main attractions for WordPress users is the great themes contributed by the thousands of users around the world. Some of these themes are proprietary and some are free. Using these themes, you can decorate and display your WordPress blog in whatever style you want. Though in general bloggers are happy with customized themes, sometimes to make something different from others, you may want to customize the look and feel of your blog. If that is so, there is no way other than editing the theme files.

In this chapter, we will show you how to develop WordPress themes on your own. We will also show you some quick tricks to achieve the desired functionality by editing the minimum amount of code. Design hacks and directions will help you to develop awesome themes for the rest of the WordPress community.

Just keep in mind that creating a WordPress theme doesn't require you to be a PHP pro. All you need is a basic idea about PHP, loops, and variables. Sometimes even just a cut-copy-paste will work fine. The most important thing that you need is a good knowledge about CSS.

Start Using a Blank Page

Before going deep into theme development, we need to understand how WordPress actually works and how the contents are served to the end users. So we will start with a blank theme (a blank PHP file) and play with it. Once you get the basic idea, we will dive into further details.

Set It Up

Using your favorite text editor or PHP editor, create a blank PHP file inside the **themes** folder. WordPress themes have a lot of code in CSS and a minimal amount of code in PHP. A theme consists of at least one CSS file and a couple of PHP files.

To set up a blank theme, we need to create two files first and then we will grow gradually. So how do you want to name your theme? Choose an interesting name, because the WordPress community will know you by the name of your theme. For the time being, let our theme be known as "zephyr".

Every theme must stay in its own directory, and you must place each theme under the **themes** folder inside the wp-content/themes folder. Let us create a folder "zephyr" under the **themes** folder.

Inside this **zephyr** folder (wp-content/themes/zephyr), we will now create a CSS file by the name of style.css in which we will define our theme for the WordPress blogging engine (it may sound a bit weird, but that is easy). Let us create the CSS file with the following content:

```
/*
Theme Name: Zephyr
Theme URI: http://our_wordpress_url
Description: Some description about our theme
Version: 1
Author: Its You
Author URI: http://author_website_url
*/
```

This content must be at the top of the CSS file.

Now create a blank index.php file in the same folder. Just keep it blank with absolutely no code in it.

That's it; we have developed our first theme. If you don't believe it, just log into the WordPress admin panel and click on the **Presentation** menu. At the bottom of the page, you will find our theme **zephyr** listed there.

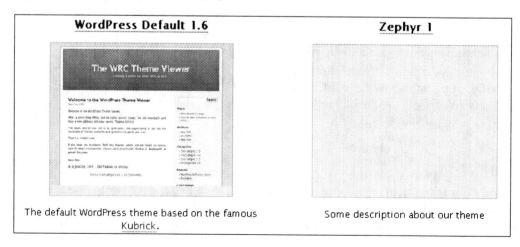

WordPress Default 1.6	Zephyr 1
The default WordPress theme based on the famous Kubrick.	Some description about our theme

If you select this theme and go to your WordPress blog, you will find a blank page. This is because we didn't add any code in our index file. The following sections will show you how to do this.

Adding Content to Our Theme

Now it's time to add some content to our theme. Let us display the title of all our posts. Open your index.php file inside the **zephyr** folder and add the following code:

```php
<?php
if (have_posts())
{
  the_post();
  the_title();
}
?>
```

This code is totally self-explanatory. It means that if there are posts in our blog, we have to fetch them and display the titles. Please note that the content of the post is fetched by the the_post() function, which is a built-in function in WordPress. Now go to your blog and run it. You will be able to see only one title, which is from our last post. Clearly this is not what we were expecting. We wanted to see the titles of all our posts. To do this, we have to just add a loop.

```php
<?php
if (have_posts())
{
  while(have_posts())
  {
    the_post();
    the_title();
    echo "<br/>";
  }
}
?>
```

The preceding code works by checking whether there are posts, and if so looping through them, fetching their content, and displaying the title. Now take a look at the blog. You will see something like the following screen:

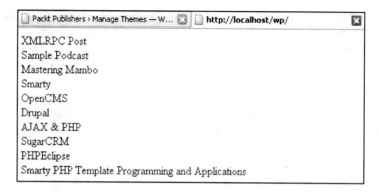

It is interesting to note that we displayed all these titles with just nine lines of code. Let's have some fun now. Each and every post in WordPress has an ID. We will now add a link to each of these titles. We will also see the content of the posts when the respective titles are clicked.

```
<?if (have_posts()):?>
  <? while(have_posts()):?>
    <? the_post()?>
    <a href='<?=the_permalink()?>'><?=the_title()?></a>
    <br/>
  <?endwhile;?>
<?endif;?>
```

Please note how we use the block syntax here for if and while loops. If you are not familiar with this syntax, please visit the alternative syntax for control structures in the PHP manual, which is available online at
http://www.php.net/manual/en/
control-structures.alternative-syntax.php.

If you now visit the blog, you will find that every title is displayed as a text link; however, nothing happens when we click on them. To further modify it, we will add some more code so that we can see the content when we click on these titles.

```
<?if (have_posts()):?>
  <? while(have_posts()):?>
    <? the_post()?>
    <a href='<?=the_permalink()?>'><?=the_title()?></a>
    <?if (!is_home()):?>
    <p>
       <?the_content();?>
```

```
    </p>
    <?endif;?>
    <br/>
  <?endwhile;?>
<?endif;?>
```

Now if you click on any title, you will see the content of that particular post.

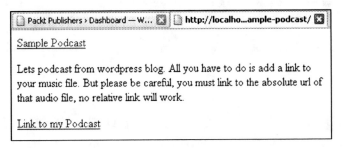

Please note that an **Edit** link is also available if you are logged in as the administrator.

Next we are going to add the category name and modify the look and feel of this page. So far WordPress has been displaying our posts using only one file, `index.php`. If we want to modify the look and feel for just the single-post display as shown in the preceding screenshot, then we can add some code in the `index.php` file; however, it is a wise idea to split the code into multiple files for the sake of manageability. WordPress seeks a file called `single.php` for displaying a single post and if that is not available, WordPress uses the `index.php` file. We are now going to add the following code to the `single.php` file to display the post with a better look and feel:

```
<? if (have_posts()) : while (have_posts()) : the_post(); ?>
  <h2><? the_title(); ?></h2>
  <? the_content(); ?>
  <? edit_post_link(__('Edit'), '<p>', '</p>'); ?>
<? endwhile; endif; ?>
```

If you now browse any post, you will view it in the following format:

Displaying the Post Excerpt on the Front Page

We displayed just the title of our posts on our front page. To display the excerpt under each post title, let us modify our front page as follows:

```
<?if (have_posts()):?>
  <? while(have_posts()):?>
    <? the_post()?>
    <a href='<?=the_permalink()?>'><?=the_title()?></a>
      <?the_content("more");?>
    <br/>
  <?endwhile;?>
<?endif;?>
```

The <the_content("more")> function will split the post content and display the portion before the <more> tag placed inside the post, if any is available.

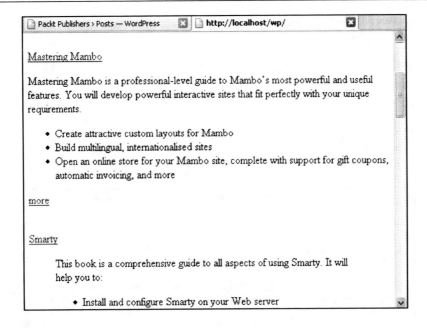

Please note the **more** link displayed in the preceding screenshot.

Retrieving the Category Name for Each Post

If we want to display on the front page the category name under which a post belongs, let us modify the code in the index.php file as follows:

```
<?if (have_posts()):?>
  <? while(have_posts()):?>
    <? the_post()?>
    <a href='<?=the_permalink()?>'><?=the_title()?></a>
    in <strong><?the_category(",");?></strong>
      <?the_content("more");?>
    <br/>
  <?endwhile;?>
<?endif;?>
```

Now if you browse the front page, it will display the category names beside all the posts.

Retrieving the Date and Author

Again, we may want to display the date and author of each post beneath the post title. The WordPress API contains all the necessary functions for themes, and we have built-in functions for displaying the name and author of each post as well. Let us modify the single.php file as follows:

```
<?if (have_posts()):?>
  <? while(have_posts()):?>
    <? the_post()?>
    <h1><a href='<?=the_permalink()?>'><?=the_title()?></a></h1>
    <?php _e("Posted "); ?> by <?php the_author() ?> at
                                    <?php the_time('F jS, Y')?><hr/>
      <?the_content("more");?>
    <br/>
  <?endwhile;?>
<?endif;?>
```

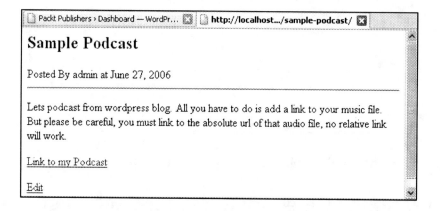

Retrieving Lists of Categories, Archives, and Calendars

There are several ways in which you can sort your blog posts, for example, through categories and archives. You can also display a calendar where all the posts are linked by dates; so whenever you click on any date, you can see all the posts made on that day. The WordPress API has built-in functions for all these.

To retrieve the list of categories, you can use the `wp_list_cats()` function. While using this function, you can exclude some categories and sort them according to different criteria. For example, take a look at the following code:

```
<?
//this will display all categories
wp_list_cats();
echo "<hr>";
//this will display all available categories excluding some specified
//exclusively
wp_list_cats("exclude=2,5,1,6&sort_column=name");
?>
```

If you run this code in the index.php file, you will understand the difference.

To display the archive of your posts, use the wp_get_archives() function. You can display archives in the following formats:

- Monthly
- Daily
- PostByPost
- Weekly

You can limit the length of the archive by supplying an additional limit parameter. You can also enclose each archive link by supplying before and after parameters.

```
<? wp_get_archives('type=monthly&limit=5'); ?>
```

Take a look at the different archiving styles as shown in the following screenshot:

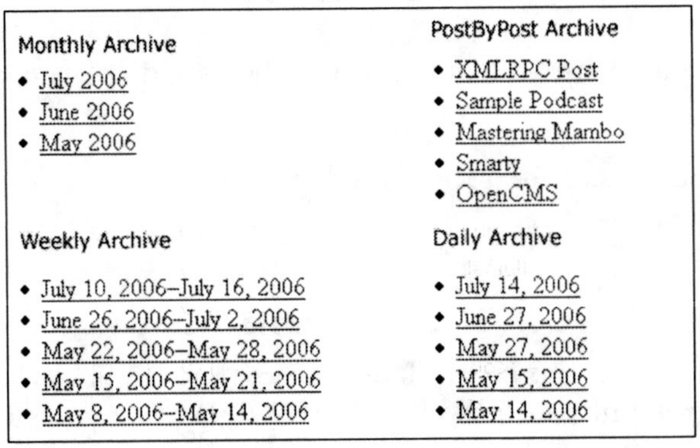

Monthly Archive

- July 2006
- June 2006
- May 2006

PostByPost Archive

- XMLRPC Post
- Sample Podcast
- Mastering Mambo
- Smarty
- OpenCMS

Weekly Archive

- July 10, 2006–July 16, 2006
- June 26, 2006–July 2, 2006
- May 22, 2006–May 28, 2006
- May 15, 2006–May 21, 2006
- May 8, 2006–May 14, 2006

Daily Archive

- July 14, 2006
- June 27, 2006
- May 27, 2006
- May 15, 2006
- May 14, 2006

You can display a calendar in your WordPress blog using the wp_get_calendar() function.

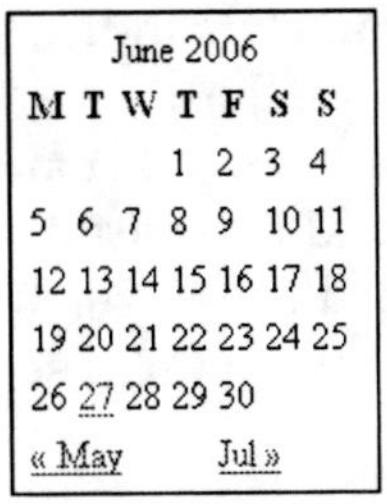

```
        June 2006
M  T  W  T  F  S  S
             1  2  3  4
 5  6  7  8  9 10 11
12 13 14 15 16 17 18
19 20 21 22 23 24 25
26 27 28 29 30
« May        Jul »
```

The date on which a post was made will be shown as a link so that anyone can click it and view the posts.

Display an RSS Feed Image beside Every Category

If you want to display the RSS feed link for each of the categories, you just need to specify the feed image in the `wp_list_cats()` function. For example, take a look at the following code block:

```
<?
wp_list_cats("exclude=2,5,1,6&sort_column=name&feed_image=feed.gif");
?>
```

When you run the code (assuming you have placed a small RSS icon, `feed.gif`, in your WordPress root folder), you will see the following output:

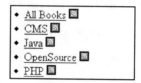

Since we haven't defined any style for links yet, they are displayed in the default format.

All the category parameters are documented in detail in `http://codex.wordpress.org`.

Displaying Blogroll and Pagelinks

To display all the links in your blogroll, use the `wp_get_links()` function. It will deliver all the blogroll links enclosed by any HTML tag that you supply.

```
<?php get_links('-1', '<li>', '</li>', '', 0, 'name', 0, 0, -1, 0, true); ?>
```

The preceding line of code will display links from your blogroll under every category. The second and third parameters indicate the HTML tags that are to be used to wrap each of these links. Here, the `<li>` and `</li>` parameters mean that they will output links in the `<li><a href='linkurl'>linktext</a></li>` format. The sixth parameter indicates the field to be used to sort the links. The last parameter is a very interesting one. We supplied `true`, which indicates that the function will output the links on the page. If we supplied `false`, it would have returned the output instead of displaying it.

Almost every WordPress core function has the capability of either displaying the output or returning it to the calling procedure. If you plan to process the returned output, then capturing the output is necessary.

To display the links of the available pages, use the `wp_list_pages()` function. You can supply the title to be displayed as shown below.

```
<? wp_list_pages("title_li=MyPages")?>
```

Displaying Blog Information

You may also want to display some basic information about your blog in your theme. This information could be your `admin_email`, `rss_url`, `atom_url`, `pingback_url`, or `comments_url`.

To display all or some of this information, you need to invoke only one function, which is `bloginfo()`. Let us see the following example:

```
<a href='<?bloginfo('rss_url')?>'>RSS</a><br/>
<a href='<?bloginfo('rss2_url')?>'>RSS2</a><br/>
<a href='<?bloginfo('atom_url')?>'>Atom</a><br/>
<a href='<?bloginfo('comments_rss2_url')?>'>CommentsRSS</a><br/>
```

This code will produce the following HTML output, specific to my blog settings.

```
<a href="http://localhost/wp/feed/rss/">RSS</a><br>
<a href="http://localhost/wp/feed/">RSS2</a><br>
<a href="http://localhost/wp/feed/atom/">Atom</a><br>
<a href="http://localhost/wp/comments/feed/">CommentsRSS</a><br>
```

Since I am running the blog example from my PC, the URL is localhost. However, it will vary from blog to blog.

There are several other parameters available that can be passed to `bloginfo`. These parameters are needed while developing plug-ins and themes where you need information to access specific files.

These parameters are `wpurl`, `siteurl`, `description`, `name`, `pingback_url`, `stylesheet_url`, `stylesheet_directory`, `template_directory`, `admin_email`, `charset`, and `version`.

Displaying a Search Bar

A search bar is a essential part in the sidebar. If we want to display a search bar in our theme, we need to add the following code in our sidebar file, `sidebar.php`:

```
<li id="search">
  <?php include (TEMPLATEPATH . '/searchform.php'); ?>
</li>
```

The preceding code includes a file named `searchform.php` from our current theme directory. This `searchform.php` file includes the following block of code:

```
<form method="get" action="<?php echo $_SERVER['PHP_SELF']; ?>">
<p>
<input type="text" value="<?php echo wp_specialchars($s, 1); ?>"
name="s" id="s" />
<input type="submit" value=" Search " />
</p>
</form>
```

Displaying Comments under Each Post

We are now going to display a section for adding comments under each post, especially in single-post mode. When a visitor clicks over a post title, then he or she can read the post content, read the existing comments, and post his or her comments.

For displaying the comment submission form and the existing comments, we need to place code in a new file, `comments.php`. The following section explain this.

Displaying Existing Comments

Let us modify our `comments.php` file as follows. We will first check for available comments and display them, if any. If commenting is open for this post, we will also display an RSS feed for the comments and a trackback URL for this post.

```
<?php if ( $comments ) : ?>
<ol id="commentlist">

<?php foreach ($comments as $comment) : ?>
  <li id="comment-<?php comment_ID() ?>">
  <?php comment_text() ?>
  <p><cite><?php comment_type(__('Comment'), __('Trackback'), __
('Pingback')); ?>
  <?php _e('by'); ?>
  <?php comment_author_link() ?> &#8212;
  <?php comment_date() ?> @
```

```
    <a href="#comment-<?php comment_ID() ?>">
    <?php comment_time() ?>
    </a></cite> <?php edit_comment_link(__("Edit This"), ' |'); ?></p>
    </li>

<?php endforeach; ?>

<?php else : // If no comment is available ?>
    <p><?php _e('No comments.'); ?></p>
<?php endif; ?>
```

Now if you visit the page, you will find the screen looking as follows:

Sample Podcast

Posted By admin at June 27, 2006

Lets podcast from wordpress blog. All you have to do is add a link to your music file. But please be careful, you must link to the absolute url of that audio file, no relative link will work.

Link to my Podcast

No comments yet.

RSS feed for comments on this post. | TrackBack URI

Now add the following section in your `comments.php` file to enable visitors to make comments.

```
<? if ( comments_open() ) : ?>
<form action="<? echo get_option('siteurl'); ?>/wp-comments-post.php"
method="post" id="commentform">

<? if ( $user_ID ) : ?>

<p>Logged in as <a href="<? echo get_option('siteurl'); ?>/wp-admin/
profile.php"><? echo $user_identity; ?></a>. <a href="<? echo get_
option('siteurl'); ?>/wp-login.php?action=logout" title="<? _e('Log
out of this account') ?>">Logout &raquo;</a></p>

<? else : ?>

<p><input type="text" name="author" id="author" value="<? echo
$comment_author; ?>" size="22" tabindex="1" />
<label for="author"><small>Name <? if ($req) _e('(required)'); ?></
small></label></p>

<p><input type="text" name="email" id="email" value="<? echo $comment_
author_email; ?>" size="22" tabindex="2" />
```

```
<label for="email"><small>Mail (will not be published) <? if ($req)
_e('(required)'); ?></small></label></p>

<p><input type="text" name="url" id="url" value="<? echo $comment_
author_url; ?>" size="22" tabindex="3" />
<label for="url"><small>Website</small></label></p>

<? endif; ?>

<p><textarea name="comment" id="comment" cols="100%" rows="10"
tabindex="4"></textarea></p>

<p><input name="submit" type="submit" id="submit" tabindex="5"
value="Submit Comment" />
<input type="hidden" name="comment_post_ID" value="<? echo $id; ?>" />
</p>
<? do_action('comment_form', $post->ID); ?>

</form>
<? endif; ?>
```

Now if you visit the page, you will see the following output:

Sample Podcast

Posted By admin at June 27, 2006

Lets podcast from wordpress blog. All you have to do is add a link to your music file. But please be careful, you must link to the absolute url of that audio file, no relative link will work.

Link to my Podcast

No comments yet.

RSS feed for comments on this post. | TrackBack URI

	Name (required)
	Mail (will not be published) (required)
	Website

Submit Comment

We have discussed all the basic things you need to know for kick-starting theme development. We will now create a nice theme for ourselves with all these features and having a good look and feel.

Plan for a Design

Before creating a theme, always have a clear idea about the look and the features of your theme. WordPress themes can be of one-column, two columns, three columns, or four columns. Among these, one-column and two-column themes are the most common and popular as opposed to four-column themes.

Please note that table-based layout designs are not a good idea for designing layouts. Try to use <div> object and CSS for layout design. This will give you extreme flexibility over your themes.

In this chapter, we will cover a typical two-column theme since it is impossible to cover every type of layout. However, we will also cover the layout code for three-column and four-column themes. A two-column theme could be either of the following two; that is, we can have our sidebar either on the left or the right side.

Out of the preceding two layouts, we will design the first one here. However, it is not a big issue to convert our design to the second one.

In the sidebar, we will display categories, recent comments, recent posts, a calendar, a search bar, a login link, a blogroll, and some introductory text. We will also fetch RSS feeds from outside and display them in our sidebar.

In the header section, we will display our blog title and an image.

In the footer section, we will display some RSS links and copyright information.

Later in this chapter, we will also discuss widget-enabled themes and how to add several options in the administration panel. We will start by creating the CSS code for our layout and design in a single `index.php` and `style.css` file. Gradually, we will split the components. Our theme will be Opera-, IE_, and Firefox-compatible.

CSS and HTML Code for a Two-Column Theme

As we start with a blank `index.php` file, we will not insert any PHP code at first. Let us make a simple `index.php` file with the following code:

```
<!DOCTYPE html PUBLIC "-//W3C//DTD XHTML 1.0 Transitional//EN"
"http://www.w3.org/TR/xhtml1/DTD/xhtml1-transitional.dtd">
<html xmlns="http://www.w3.org/1999/xhtml">
<head>
<meta http-equiv="Content-Type" content="text/html; charset=iso-8859-
1" />
<title>Untitled Document</title>
</head>
<style>
  div
  {
    border: 1px solid #ccc;
  }
  body
  {
    margin:0px;
    margin-top: 10px;
  }
  #container
  {
    width: 900px;
    margin:auto;
    border: 0px solid #ccc;
  }

  #header
  {
    height: 100px;
  }

  #post_container
  {
    border: 0px solid #ccc;
  }

  .separator
```

```
{
  clear:both;
  margin-top: 10px;
  margin-bottom:5px;
  border: 0px solid #ccc;
}

#left_pan, #right_pan
{
  float: left;
  height: 400px;
}

#left_pan
{
  width: 200px;
}

#right_pan
{
  width: 690px;
  margin-left: 5px;
}

#footer
{
  clear: both;
  height: 20px;
}

</style>
<body>
<div id="container">
  <div id="header">
  </div>
  <div class="separator">
  </div>
  <div id="post_container">
    <div id="left_pan">
    </div>

    <div id="right_pan">
    </div>
    <div class="separator">
    </div>
  </div>
```

```
    <div class="separator">
    </div>
  <div id="footer">
  </div>
</div>

</body>
</html>
```

The code marked as bold in the preceding file is redundant. This is just to demonstrate how CSS-based layout actually works. In our original theme, we will remove these lines.

Now if you browse the page, you will see the following output:

The layout is same in Firefox, IE, and Opera. If you want your sidebar on the right side, just change the CSS code in the preceding file as follows and your sidebar will instantly move to the right.

```
#left_pan
  {
    width: 690px;
  }

#right_pan
  {
    width: 200px;
```

```
margin-left: 5px;
}
```

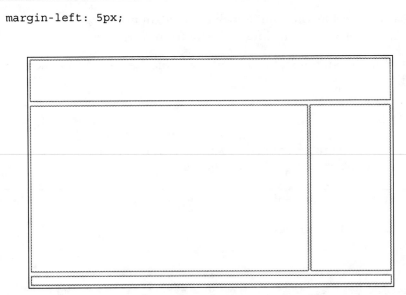

So you now understand why CSS-based layouts are so widely used. They are easy to maintain, easy to modify, and of course flexible to work with.

Next, we will split our theme into smaller parts for the sake of maintainability. For example, we will split our theme into four parts:

- Header
- Body
- Sidebar
- Footer

Let us modify our index.php file as follows:

```
<?php  get_header(); ?>
  <div id="post_container">
    <?php get_sidebar(); ?>
    <div id="right_pan">
    </div>
    <div class="separator">
    </div>
<?php get_footer(); ?>
```

You may wonder about the small size of the previously big index.php file. Well, the other parts of the file are distributed among four files: style.css, header.php, sidebar.php, and footer.php. The built-in function get_header() includes the content in header.php in the current directory (that is our theme directory).

`get_sidebar()` does the same, but it includes content from
`sidebar.php`; `get_footer()` includes content from `footer.php`.

We moved out all style content to the `style.css` file. Let us now see the content for the other files.

header.php

```
<!DOCTYPE html PUBLIC "-//W3C//DTD XHTML 1.0 Transitional//EN"
"http://www.w3.org/TR/xhtml1/DTD/xhtml1-transitional.dtd">
<html xmlns="http://www.w3.org/1999/xhtml">
<head>
<meta http-equiv="Content-Type" content="text/html; charset=iso-8859-
1" />
<title>Untitled Document</title>
</head>

  <style type="text/css" media="screen">
    @import url( <?php bloginfo('stylesheet_url'); ?> );
  </style>

<body>
<div id="container">
  <div id="header">
  </div>
  <div class="separator">
  </div>
```

sidebar.php

```
    <div id="left_pan">
    </div>
```

footer.php

```
  </div>
    <div class="separator">
    </div>
  <div id="footer">
  </div>
</div>

</body>
</html>
```

We have split our `index.php` file into four small parts. Here, we see three parts, namely `header.php`, `sidebar.php`, and `footer.php`. The `index.php` file will itself contain another part that is the body. Since the body is quite large, we will create it step-by-step later in the chapter. All the four parts are included together in the `index.php` file; so the output remains same. We split our code into four separate files so that we can design each part more conveniently.

Design the Header

Now it's time to design our header. Open the `header.php` file in your favorite text editor. We need to see the blog title and the blog subtitle in the header. Besides, we also need a header image.

We need to create a nice background for our header section; so we create a 5*150 pixel GIF file with a gradient effect. We save that file as `bg.gif` in the **images** folder under our **themes** folder.

Let us now code our `header.php` file as follows:

```
<!DOCTYPE html PUBLIC "-//W3C//DTD XHTML 1.0 Transitional//EN"
"http://www.w3.org/TR/xhtml1/DTD/xhtml1-transitional.dtd">
<html xmlns="http://www.w3.org/1999/xhtml">
<head>
<meta http-equiv="Content-Type" content="text/html;
                                    charset=iso-8859-1" />
<title>Untitled Document</title>
</head>
  <style type="text/css" media="screen">
    @import url( <?php bloginfo('stylesheet_url'); ?> );
  </style>

<body>
<div id="container">
  <div id="header">
    <div id="header_title">
      <?php bloginfo('name'); ?>
    </div>
    <div id="header_subtitle">
      <?php bloginfo('description'); ?>
    </div>
  </div>
  <div class="separator">
  </div>
```

We will also add the following CSS code to our `style.css` file:

```
#header
{
```

```
    height: 150px;
    background-image: url("images/bg.gif");
    border: 1px solid #000;

}

#header_title
{
  font-family:Georgia;
  font-size: 28px;
  margin-top: 45px;
  margin-left: 20px;
  color: #eee;
}
#header_subtitle
{
  font-family:Georgia;
  font-size: 12px;
  margin-top: 5px;
  margin-left: 22px;
  color: #edc;
}
```

Our page now looks as follows:

Design the Sidebar

We need to place the following content in our sidebar:

- Some description
- Pages
- Categories
- Archives
- Blogrolls (links)
- RSS links

We know how to fetch this content; so let us open the `sidebar.php` file and modify it as follows:

```
<div id="left_pan">
  <div class="sidebar_container">
    <ul>
      <li><h2>About</h2></li>
      <li>Packt publishing is a great publisher. Packt publishing is a
great publisher. Packt publishing is a great publisher.</li>
    </ul>
  </div>

    <div class="sidebar_container">
    <ul>
      <li><h2>Pages</h2></li>
      <?php wp_list_pages('title_li='); ?>
    </ul>
  </div>

  <div class="sidebar_container">
    <ul>
      <li><h2>Categories</h2></li>
      <?php wp_list_cats("exclude=2,5,1,6&sort_column=name"); ?>
    </ul>
  </div>

  <div class="sidebar_container">
    <ul>
      <li><h2>Archives</h2></li>
      <?php wp_get_archives();?>
    </ul>
  </div>

  <div class="sidebar_container">
    <ul>
      <li><h2>Links</h2></li>
      <?php wp_get_links();?>
    </ul>
  </div>

  <div class="sidebar_container">
    <ul>
      <li><h2>Meta</h2></li>
      <li><?php wp_loginout(); ?></li>

      <li><a href="<?php bloginfo('rss2_url'); ?>">RSS</a></li>
      <li><a href="http://wordpress.org/">WP</a></li>
    </ul>
  </div>
</div>
```

Let us also modify the CSS code for our sidebar as follows:

```css
#left_pan
{
  padding-left: 2px;
  padding-right: 2px;
  padding-bottom: 2px;
  padding-top: 2px;
}

#left_pan h2
{
  margin-top: 0px;
  padding-top: 2px;
  margin-bottom: 10px;
  font-size: 16px;
  padding-bottom: 5px;
  display: block;
  border-bottom: 1px solid #ccc;
  color: #8CBFF8;
}

#left_pan ul
{
  padding:0px;
  margin: 0px; /* for IE */
  list-style:none;
}

.sidebar_container
{
  padding-left: 10px;
  padding-right: 10px;
  padding-top: 5px;
  padding-bottom: 5px;
  background-color: #093C76;
  color: #eee;
}

#left_pan a:link, #left_pan a:hover, #left_pan a:visited
{
  color: #eee;
  text-decoration: none;
}
```

```
#left_pan a:hover
{
  text-decoration: underline;
}
```

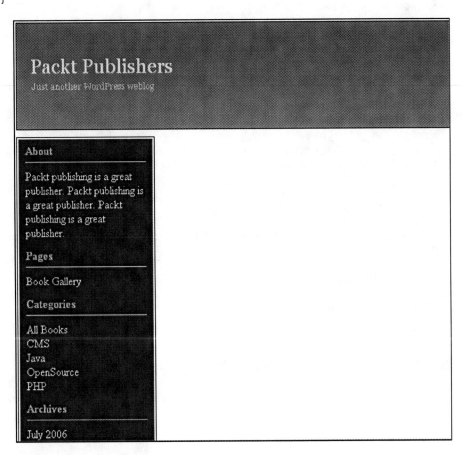

Design the Body

We have now reached the most crucial part of our blog. We need to design the body of our blog. We need to display the post title, the post author, the date on which the post was made, the post excerpt, and the number of comments. Let us first design the body. Open the `index.php` file and modify it as follows:

```php
<?php get_header(); ?>
  <div id="post_container">
    <?php get_sidebar(); ?>
    <div id="right_pan">
    <?php if (have_posts()) : while (have_posts()) : the_post(); ?>
```

```
      <div id="post-<?php the_ID(); ?>">
      <h2><a href="<?php the_permalink() ?>">
      <?php the_title(); ?></a></h2>
      <div class="meta">
      <?php _e("Posted in"); ?>
        <?php the_category(',') ?> by <?php the_author() ?> on the
        <?php the_time('F jS, Y') ?>
      <?php edit_post_link( __('Edit This')); ?></div>
      <div class="main">
      <?php the_content( __('(more...)')); ?>
      </div>
      </div>
      <div class="comments">
        <?php wp_link_pages(); ?>
        <?php comments_popup_link( __('<strong>0</strong> Comments'), __
('<strong>1</strong> Comment'), __('<strong>%</strong> Comments')); ?>
      </div>
      <?php comments_template(); ?>
      <?php endwhile; else: ?>
      <div class="warning">
        <p><?php _e('Sorry, no posts matched your criteria, please try
and search again.'); ?></p>
      </div>
      <?php endif; ?>
      </div>
      <div class="separator">
   </div>
<?php get_footer(); ?>
```

The CSS code for the `style.css` file is as follows:

```
#right_pan
{
  padding-left: 10px;
}


#right_pan h2
{
  margin-top: 0px;
  font-size: 18px;
  display: block;
  margin-bottom: 5px;

}


#right_pan .meta
{
  font-size: 12px;
```

```
    padding-bottom: 5px;
    border-bottom: 1px solid #ABB9C8;
}

#right_pan a:hover, #right_pan a:link, #right_pan a:visited
{
    text-decoration: none;
    color: #27486E;
}

#right_pan .comments
{
    padding-bottom: 20px;
}
```

After adding the body, our page will look as follows:

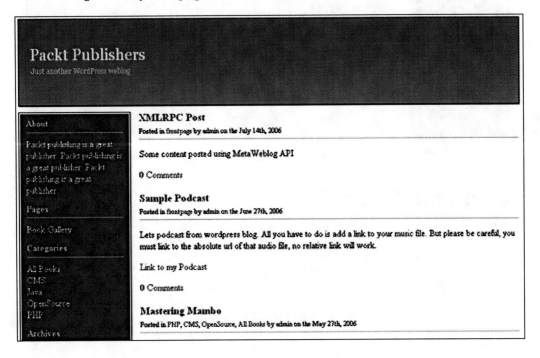

When someone selects a single post, the screen will look as follows:

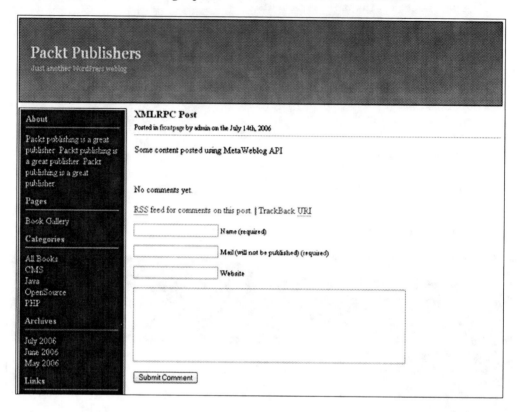

Design the Footer

This is the simplest part of our theme. Here is the code for `footer.php`:

```
    </div>
      <div class="separator">
      </div>
    <div id="footer">
      sample theme for wordpress book. powered by wordpress.
    </div>
  </div>
  </body>
  </html>
```

The code for `style.css` is as follows:

```
/* footer */
#footer{
```

```
    border-top: 1px solid #ccc;
    padding-top: 20px;
    padding-bottom: 20px;
    font-size: 12px;
}
```

Themes in Minutes

In the previous section, we learned how to create themes from scratch. We had ultimate flexibility over our design and created exactly what we wanted. However, all this comes at a cost. To develop a theme completely from scratch needs a lot of time.

Recall how we started our theme development process. We first planned our theme, thought over its design, and probably sketched roughly with some illustration software. Finally, after fixing the design and content, we started coding. You should not self-design a theme unless you are delivering a very complex theme like the one http://www.ajaxian.com has. If you go to the Ajaxian website, you will find a lot of gadgets there and it represents its content in a very nice and stylish way.

For creating quick themes, you can pick an already existing theme that is similar to your planned design (at least in terms of layout) and modify its code. Sometimes these themes are so similar to each other that all you need to do is edit the CSS file.

Ian Marine's very popular Green Marine theme is a very interesting theme with a lot of work around. This theme comes in different color schemes obtained just by modifying its CSS file and sometimes slightly changing the image files. For example, there are two variations of the Green Marine theme created by Ian Marine. They are called Blue Marine and Orange Marine, respectively.

These two variations will help you to understand that you can bring considerable changes to the look and feel of the theme by modifying the CSS file.

There is one more trick for instantly getting a suitable theme for yourself. Many of these themes have built-in banner images. You can modify these banners and get a native look for your site. If you are not sure where to find these banner images, you can search for the **images** folder inside the theme folder. Usually theme developers use this **images** folder to store the images relevant to themes. If that doesn't work, you can search the image files inside the theme folder one by one or directly go to header.php and see where the banner image has been taken from.

You can go to http://codex.wordpress.org to look for some appropriate themes for your site. There you will find some popular WordPress theme repositories.

Instant Theme Builders

Besides editing existing themes and developing from scratch, you can also obtain themes using theme builders. Theme builders are web-based or desktop-based applications where you can specify colors, layouts, and other styles for the different parts of a theme (namely, header, sidebar, body, and footer).You can then generate CSS files accordingly.

The most advanced instant theme builder is available at:
`http://redalt.com/tools/builder.php`.

Step 1: Select the Layout

In the theme builder by RedAlt, there are four supported layouts. You can select any of the four layout styles. Take a look at the following screenshot overleaf:

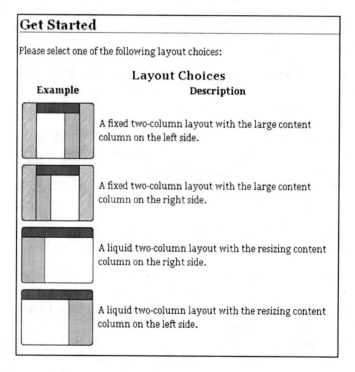

Step 2: Select Some Options

In this step, you can select some options for the different sections, like whether you want to display RSS Links, Trackback links, and so forth.

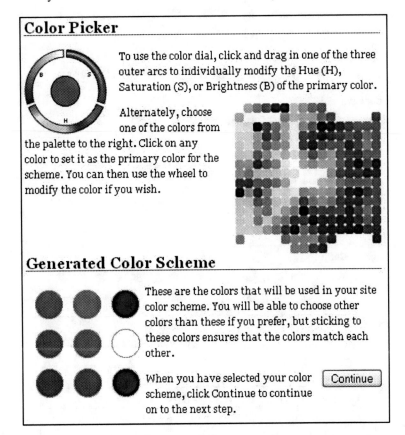

Step 3: Select a Color Scheme

This step allows you to select a basic color scheme for your theme.

Color Picker

To use the color dial, click and drag in one of the three outer arcs to individually modify the Hue (H), Saturation (S), or Brightness (B) of the primary color.

Alternately, choose one of the colors from the palette to the right. Click on any color to set it as the primary color for the scheme. You can then use the wheel to modify the color if you wish.

Generated Color Scheme

These are the colors that will be used in your site color scheme. You will be able to choose other colors than these if you prefer, but sticking to these colors ensures that the colors match each other.

When you have selected your color scheme, click Continue to continue on to the next step.

[Continue]

Step 4: Details of Colors and Download

In this step, you can specify the color details for the different sections.

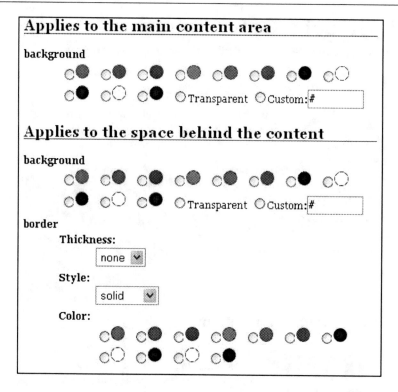

Finally, you can download the theme by clicking on the **Download** link at the bottom of the page.

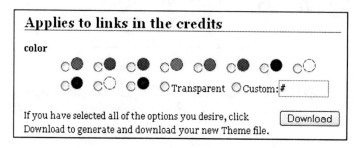

After downloading, you can use this theme file as usual.

Widgetizing Themes

In WordPress 2.0, there is a plug-in called **widget**, which is an interesting part of WordPress. This plug-in has been developed by Automatic.com where the developer of WordPress, Matt Mullenweg also works. Using this plug-in, you can dynamically customize your sidebar by dragging and dropping widgets. Widgets are small dragable parts that handle different types of functionality in the WordPress blog. For example, a Text Widget helps to display some text; an RSS widget fetches RSS contents from remote sites, and so forth.

In a standard widget plug-in, there are six types of built-in widgets. However, there are a lot of third-party widgets also. Let us see how to manage these widgets.

Log into the WordPress admin panel and select any theme from the **Presentation** menu. If that theme is "widget-ready" or compatible with widgets, you will instantly find a sub-menu called **Sidebar Widgets** available under the **Presentation** menu.

If you select the **Sidebar Widgets** menu, you will find something like the following:

Now you can drag each of these items onto your sidebar (on the right) and your sidebar will contain only those items. For example, let us drag three widgets: recent posts, recent comments, and a text widget. If you click on the icon on the right-hand side of each widget, you can configure that widget.

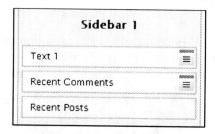

Now if you browse your blog, you will see the change in your sidebar.

Making Your Theme Widget Enabled

To make our theme widget enabled, we need to make some simple changes. Open your sidebar file and modify according to the following:

```
<div id="left_pan">
  <div class="sidebar_container">
    <ul>
    <?php if ( !function_exists('dynamic_sidebar') ||
                                    !dynamic_sidebar() ) : ?>
        <li><h2>About</h2></li>
```

```
      <li>Packt publishing is a great publisher. Packt publishing is
         a great publisher. Packt publishing is a great publisher.</li>
   </ul>
</div>
  <div class="sidebar_container">
  <ul>
     <li><h2>Pages</h2></li>
     <?php wp_list_pages('title_li='); ?>
  </ul>
</div>
<div class="sidebar_container">
  <ul>
     <li><h2>Categories</h2></li>
     <?php wp_list_cats("exclude=2,5,1,6&sort_column=name"); ?>
  </ul>
</div>
<div class="sidebar_container">
  <ul>
     <li><h2>Archives</h2></li>
     <?php wp_get_archives();?>
  </ul>
</div>
<div class="sidebar_container">
  <ul>
     <li><h2>Links</h2></li>
     <?php wp_get_links();?>
  </ul>
</div>
<div class="sidebar_container">
  <ul>
     <li><h2>Meta</h2></li>
     <li><?php wp_loginout(); ?></li>
     <li><a href="<?php bloginfo('rss2_url'); ?>">RSS</a></li>
     <li><a href="http://wordpress.org/">WP</a></li>
  <? endif;?>
  </ul>
  </div>
  <div style="azimuth:behind">
  </div>
</div>
```

Well, one last step for completion. Create a file called functions.php in our theme folder, i.e. zephyr, and add the following code in it:

```
<?
if ( function_exists('register_sidebars') )
  register_sidebars(1);
?>
```

Now if you select **zephyr** as your theme, you will find that a **Sidebar Widgets** menu appears.

Now you can drag and drop widgets from this menu. For example, make your sidebar like this:

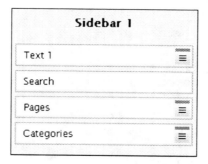

After making all the desired changes, your blog will look as follows:

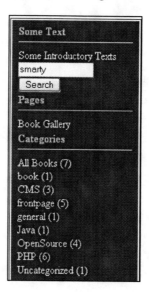

Summary

In this chapter, we learned how easy it is to develop themes according to our needs with the help of the feature-rich WordPress API. We also learned about widgets, how to use them, and how to enable our theme for widgets.

In the next chapter, we will learn about community blogging and managing user groups. Till then, have fun in playing with themes. Try to modify our theme. If you see anything interesting in any other theme, go to the code of that theme and learn how to implement that functionality in our theme.

8
Community Blogging

In the previous chapter, you learned how to manage the look and the feel of your WordPress blog by creating and modifying themes. In this chapter, we are going to introduce community blogging and user management. So far in this book we have been discussing a blog that is maintained by a single author; however, in real life this may not always make sense. There may be different communities with a set of bloggers who wish to blog at a single place, but as a separate entity.

In this chapter, we will discuss how to manage a group of authors in a single blog and how to manage their privileges. There is a special version of WordPress called WordPress MU that is developed solely as a multi-user blogging platform. WordPress MU is not officially maintained with WordPress releases. Since it is not a mainstream product, it is also not very well supported. However, it is worth being familiar with WordPress MU. This versatile multi-user blogging platform is discussed in detail in Chapter 10.

Flavors of Multi-User Blogging

WordPress is an extremely powerful blogging engine. Regular blogging requires a lot of features, some of which you discover when you require them. One of those features is multi-user blogging. Blogs are basically operated by single authors. However, there are several cases where a blog is required so that many people can blog jointly. If you are not sure, consider the following cases where a multi-user blog plays a diverse role.

A multi-user blogging platform is extremely useful for a group of people with similar interests. If that group wants to publish news on a specific topic (or on many topics in a broad sense), then there must be some facility so that they can log in as individual entities and post their content. However, in a multi-user blogging platform, content moderation is very vital. There must be some sort of moderation so that content is displayed after being approved by an authorized person.

Multi-user blogging platforms can play a vital role for developers. For example, if a group of remote developers (of a specific project) share their experiences in a blog, it will prove to be very helpful for new developers who might face similar kinds of problems. This blog may then act as a knowledge base for them.

Multi-user blogs are also helpful when used as a centralized news source or a central blogging zone for the employees of a company.

Managing Users in a Multi-User Blogging Platform

The first step of maintaining a multi-user blogging platform is to maintain a relation between the authors. All authors should not have similar privileges. There may be an author with higher privilege and power than the others. Above that author, there may be a small group of comparatively more privileged authors who act as moderators. Finally, there may be some general authors for writing and posting content frequently.

The WordPress admin panel provides everything you need to set up different privileges for these users. Let us first see how to create a user in a blog.

First of all, log into the admin panel and go to the **Users** menu. To add multiple users, select the **Authors and Users** sub-menu.

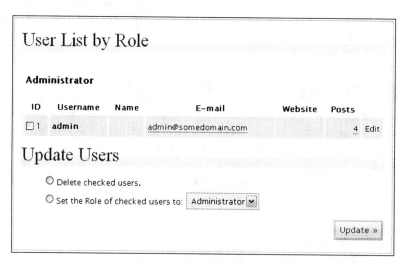

If you scroll down the page, you will find an option to add a new user to your blog. You are required to provide some basic information on this page. Let us add a user called **test** with a password **demo**.

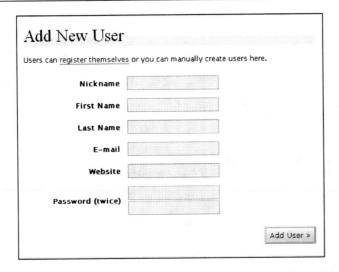

After the successful addition of a user, you will find the user added in the user panel. If you scroll down the page, you will see something like the following:

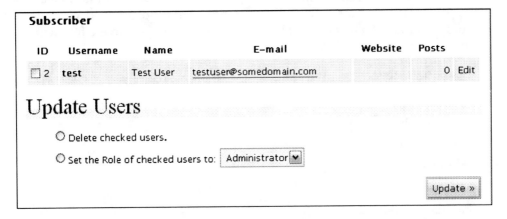

From this panel, you can set the user privileges right away by selecting their roles from the drop-down menu **Set the Role of checked users to**. Please note that all the newly added users will have the default privileges of a subscriber, which equals zero, which is the lowest in a group. A subscriber has the least privileges as compared to others. There are five different levels of privileges that you can set for a group of users or a particular user. These levels are Administrator, Editor, Author, Contributor, and Subscriber.

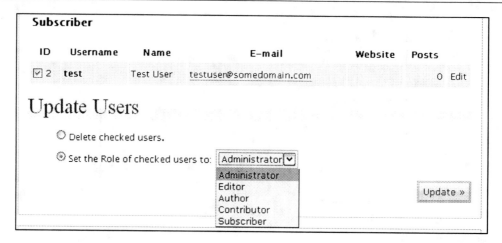

Administrator

An administrator is a person who can do everything in WordPress. There is no barrier for an administrator. As there are no permission problems for administrators, we will not be discussing more about them. However, it is not a wise decision to keep multiple administrators in one blog. An administrator can do the following jobs, which other editors can't do.

- Switch the themes
- Edit themes
- Activate any plug-in
- Edit any plug-in
- Edit users
- Edit files
- Manage options

Editor

An editor is capable of managing other people's post, moderating those posts, and finally publishing them. An editor cannot add or edit a user in WordPress. Let us see what an editor can do. First of all, let us take a look at the following screenshot. This is what an editor will see when logged into the blog.

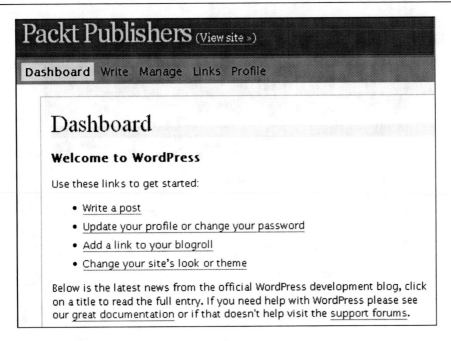

Note that an editor has fewer menus available to him or her as compared to an administrator. Besides, there are lesser options available under each menu. For example, if an editor opens the **Manage** menu, he or she will see the following options available:

An editor can manage posts and modify their content. He or she can also manage the content of the pages. He or she can add and modify the categories, manage and moderate the comments, or mark the comments as spam, if any.

When an editor goes to the **Link** section, he or she will find the following menu available to him or her:

An editor is able to manage the links and link categories. He or she can also import links from an external OPML file. Briefly, as compared to an author, an editor can do the following additional jobs.

- Moderate comments
- Manage categories
- Manage links

Author

An author is a comparatively less privileged person than an editor. When an author logs into the WordPress blog, he or she will have the following dashboard available:

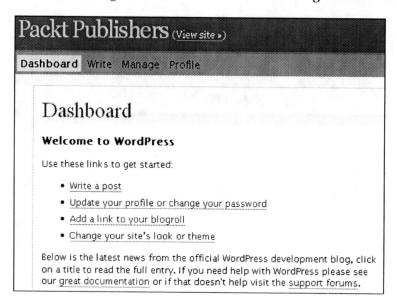

Authors can manage posts made by them or their subordinates. However, they cannot modify posts made by other authors. They cannot even modify comments made to a post that was not written by them. Authors have full freedom to modify their content, but are by no means privileged to modify others content. When authors click on the **Manage** menu, they will get the following options available:

As stated earlier, an author can only view other people's posts but cannot edit them. This is shown in the following screenshot:

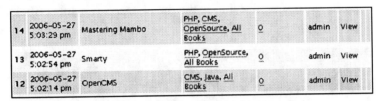

Contributor

A contributor is only able to write and submit posts. However, these posts will not be published unless they are approved by an editor, an author, or an administrator. A contributor sees the same dashboard as an author, but there are significant changes in the writing panel and the manage section. Let us take a look at the contributor's writing panel:

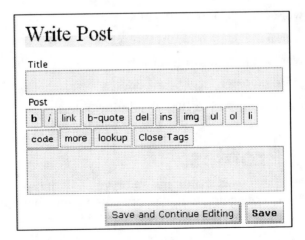

Please note that there is no **Publish** button in the writing panel. You can only save your post as a draft when you are logged in as a contributor.

Under the **Manage** menu, you will get the following options:

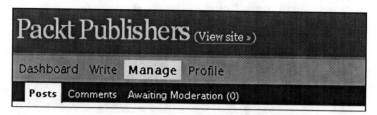

Subscriber

A subscriber can only read comments and posts. He or she can also subscribe to newsletters, if available any. Following is the dashboard for a subscriber when logged in.

User Levels

If you are using WordPress version 1.5 and have not updated to the recent version, then you may have some levels instead of these roles. There are levels from 0 to 10. Each level specifies some privilege. Let us see what these levels mean:

- One who works at level 0 is a subscriber.
- One who works at level 1 is a contributor.
- One who works at level 2 to 4 is an author.
- One who works at level 5 to 7 is an editor.
- One who works at level 8 to 10 is an administrator.

Managing Profiles

If you go to the **Profile** section as an administrator, you will find many options available to you. We are now going to have a brief discussion about the profile section.

Name		Contact Info	
Username: (no editing)		**E-mail: (required)**	
admin		admin@somedomain.com	
First name:		**Website:**	
		http://	
Last name:		**AIM:**	
Nickname:		**Yahoo IM:**	
admin			
Display name publicly as:		**Jabber / Google Talk:**	
admin			

About yourself	Update Your Password
Share a little biographical information to fill out your profile. This may be shown publicly.	If you would like to change your password type a new one twice below. Otherwise leave this blank.
	New Password:
	Type it one more time:

Personal Options

☑ Use the visual rich editor when writing

The preceding page asks you to input all the basic information about yourself. You can also update your current password by entering the new password in the bottom-right section.

An important option is available at the bottom-left of this page, namely **Use the visual rich editor when writing**. This option specifies the type of editor that will appear while writing a post in the writing panel. If you check this option, you will get a WYSIWYG editor; otherwise, a traditional plain editor.

Deleting Users

If you want to delete an existing user, you should be aware of certain issues. While deleting a user, there are chances that you accidentally delete all the posts made by that user.

To delete an existing user, just log into the admin panel and select the **Profile** menu. Select **Authors and Users** from the sub-menu. You will see all the available users in your blog. You can delete any one of them by checking the check box beside each of them and clicking the delete button at the bottom.

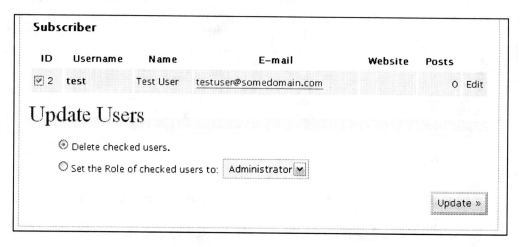

When you delete any user, the following screen appears asking you if you want to delete all the posts of that user.

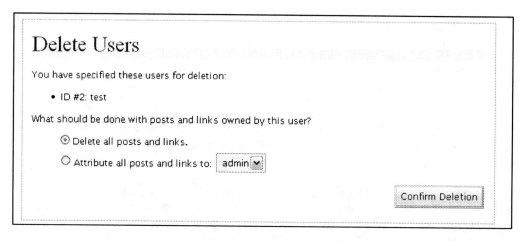

You have two options while deleting a user. You can either attribute all his or her posts to another user or you can delete all the posts made by that user. Make a choice and click on the **Confirm Deletion** button.

Restriction Plug-ins

There are several plug-ins available for setting different kinds of restriction levels in WordPress. In Codex, there are several plug-ins available for this.

Some of these plug-ins can hide portions of a WordPress post from unregistered users. Some can stick a page in the front page of WordPress and can restrict access from different IP addresses. Some allow administrators to restrict a specific post or an entire category to a group of registered users.

The WP-Members plug-in (`http://butlerblog.com/wp-members/`) turns your WordPress blog into a premium content site. It blocks content based on user login. The ViewLevel2 plug-in (`http://blog.firetree.net/2005/08/25/viewlevel-20/`) blocks posts for users below a given level. There is another plug-in called Registered–Only (`http://dev.wp-plugins.org/browser/registered-only/`), which allows only registered users to view your blog.

The HideThis plug-in (`http://edwards.org/2006/03/12/hidethis-v10-plugin-for-wordpress/`) hides a portion of the posts from non-registered users. Yet another interesting plug-in is the Freeze Users plug-in (`http://txfx.net/files/wordpress/wp_freeze_users.phps`), which blocks users from changing passwords. This is useful if your blog has a user with an open password (sandboxing) and you don't want anyone to change that password.

You can get a list of the restriction plug-ins from `http://codex.wordpress.org/Plugins/Restriction`.

Summary

In this chapter, we discussed how to manage a group of users in a single blog and hence managing a community. Community blogging can play a very important role in user groups or news sites. We also learned how to manage different levels of privileges for users in a community. In the next chapter, we will learn how to develop plug-ins and widgets.

9
Developing Plug-ins and Widgets

Plug-ins for any application are small pieces of code that work on the same framework and API as provided by the application. You may wonder about the purpose and the significance of developing plug-ins. Well, the main goal of developing plug-ins is to extend the functionality of an application. If APIs are open, any third-party developer can extend the functionality of an application by creating plug-ins. WordPress exposes a rich set of APIs through which you can extend WordPress to a higher level. Developing plug-ins for WordPress is not a tough job; all you need to have is some PHP knowledge. Developers love WordPress because of its structured and beautiful set of APIs.

Widgets are also a type of plug-in, but they are developed using the widget framework that is created by Matt Mullenweg. Matt is the lead developer of WordPress and works at Automattic. The widget framework itself is developed using the plug-in API of WordPress. The main goal of widgets is to enrich the look and feel of WordPress by providing easy-to-use, draggable objects that can take user input and display some output based on that. Widgets are developed to decorate your sidebar more easily.

The widget plug-in allows you to visually add small widgets to the sidebar of your WordPress theme from the administration panel. You can simply drag and drop your available widgets into the sidebar; each of these widgets will add a special functionality to your WordPress outlook. Almost all widgets provide greater flexibility to modify your sidebar without any hassle or coding experience. In Chapter 7, we discussed how to make your theme widget enabled.

This chapter is basically divided into two major parts. In the first part of this chapter, we will discuss the basics about widgets, installing the widget plug-in, and developing custom widgets for our themes. In the next part, we will discuss the basics of plug-in development and develop some small plug-ins to describe the process in detail.

Installing the Widget Plug-in

As explained earlier in the chapter, widgets work on the widget framework that is provided by the main widget plug-in. So our first task will be to install the widget plug-in on our WordPress blog. Firstly, download the archive of the widget plug-in from `http://www.automattic.com`. After downloading the `widgets.zip` file from `www.automattic.com`, extract it within the plug-ins folder that is inside the `wp-contents` directory inside your WordPress folder.

Now log into your WordPress admin panel and go to the **Plugins** section where you will find the widget plug-in appearing as **Sidebar Widgets**. Enable it by clicking on the **Activate** link just after the plug-in.

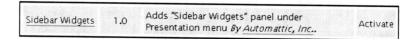

| Sidebar Widgets | 1.0 | Adds "Sidebar Widgets" panel under Presentation menu *By Automattic, Inc..* | Activate |

Creating Widgets

Widgets are basically nothing but plug-ins. However, it is important to note that widgets depend upon the widget framework and themes. Their dependence on themes is mainly because theme developers must allow the usage of widgets in their themes. As stated earlier, the main goal of widgets is decorating the sidebar in a drag-and-drop style. So if theme developers do not allow widgets in their themes, they won't work. If you have the widget plug-in installed, then after setting a new theme you will find a menu called **Sidebar Widgets** under the **Presentation** menu. If that is not available, you will know that the theme doesn't support widgets. Later in this chapter, we will discuss how you can widgetize (that means to allow the usage of widgets in) your theme.

While designing a widget, you should know that a theme has two presentation states. One is from the admin panel and the other is what visitors will see on the theme. So you have to design both of these states during coding.

In this chapter, we are going to design a widget that will display any text in the sidebar of your WordPress blog. Though you can do unlimited things with widgets, you may check what other people have done with widgets at `http://widgets.wordpress.com`.

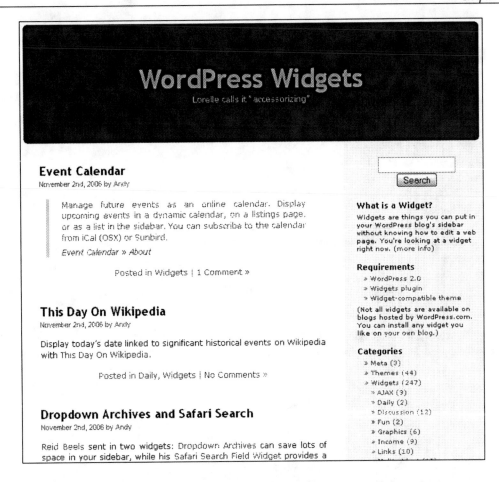

Let us now create our widget through which we can add any text in our sidebar; let us call it **Aside**. In the previous chapters of this book, we designed some small plug-ins and we know that we must add a plug-in definition at the top of our plug-in code. So we are directly going to code. However, we will dissect our code in the next section.

```
<?
/*
Plugin Name: Aside
Plugin URI: type a url
Description: a sample widget for wordpress book
Author: Hasin Hayder
Version: 1.0
Author URI: http://hasin.wordpress.com
*/
function widget_aside_init()
```

```
{
  if ( !function_exists('register_sidebar_widget') || !function_
exists('register_widget_control') )
  return;

  register_sidebar_widget('Aside', 'widget_aside_render');
  register_widget_control('Aside', 'widget_aside_admin', 350, 200);
}

function widget_aside_admin()
{
  if ($_POST['aside_submit']=='1'){
    $options['aside_title'] = $_POST['aside_title'];
    $options['aside_note'] = $_POST['aside_note'];
    update_option("widget_aside",$options);
}

  $options = get_option("widget_aside");
  if (empty($options))
  {
    $title = "Aside";
    $note = "Type your note here";
  }
  else{
    $title = $options['aside_title'];
    $note = $options['aside_note'];
  }
  echo "<div style='height: 200px'>
      <p style='text-align: left'>
      Title<br/>
      <input type='text' name='aside_title' value='{$title}'><br/>
      Note<br/>
      <textarea rows='5' cols='40' name='aside_note'>{$note}</
textarea><br/></p>
      <input type='hidden' name='aside_submit' value='1'></div>";
}

function widget_aside_render($args)
{
  extract($args);
$options = get_option("widget_aside");
  if (empty($options))
  {
    $title = "Aside";
    $note = "There is no note currently";
```

```
    }
    else {
      $title = $options['aside_title'];
      $note = $options['aside_note'];
    }
    echo $before_widget;
    echo "<li><h2>{$title}</h2></li>";
    echo "<ul><li>{$note}</li></ul>";
    echo $after_widget;
  }

  add_action('plugins_loaded', 'widget_aside_init');
  ?>
```

Let's save this widget as `aside.php` in the plug-ins directory. Now you have to activate it from the **Plugins** menu inside the administration panel. You will find this widget as **Aside** as shown in the following screenshot:

| Aside | 1.0 | a sample widget for wordpress book *By Hasin Hayder .* | Activate |

Enable this widget by clicking on the **Activate** link. After enabling it, go to the **Presentation** menu and select **Sidebar Widgets** from the sub-menu. If your theme doesn't support widgets, you will not get the **Sidebar Widgets** menu. This is the way in which you can check if your theme supports widgets.

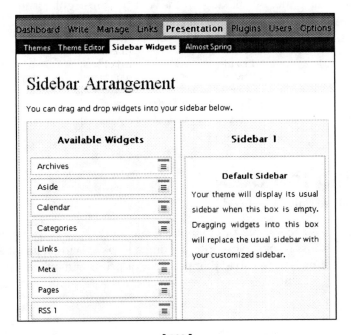

The widget named **Aside** in the left pane is the widget we just developed. Since this theme supports widgets, we can see our widget listed here in the **Available Widgets** panel. Let us drag the widget from the left pane to the right pane and click on the icon just beside it. A new panel will appear with two input boxes; one is **Title** and the other is **Note** as shown in the following screenshot. Write anything in these two boxes.

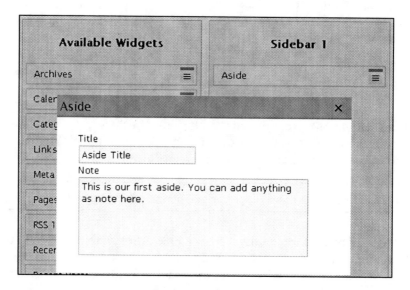

Thereafter, close this panel by clicking on the **X** at the top-right corner and scroll down. Save the changes by clicking on the **Save Changes** button. Now browse to your WordPress URL and take a look at the front page sidebar.

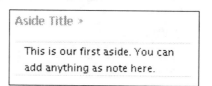

Dissecting the Code

Let us now analyze our widget code.

A widget is simply an action plug-in that hooks the loaded plug-ins. Later in this chapter we will discuss hooks. After intercepting a hook, a widget just instructs WordPress which function to run at that point. In our first widget, we created the `widget_aside_init()` function that is responsible for widget initialization.

When WordPress calls the `widget_aside_init()` function, we first check whether the widget plug-in is installed. If the widget plug-in is installed, we register our widget. As stated earlier, a widget has two presentation states; one is the admin state and the other is the display state. In the admin state, you can set different parameters and input data from the administration panel. In the display state, the widget renders some output in the sidebar that is visible to our viewers. The following two lines in our `widget_aside_init()` function are responsible for registering two functions for these two states of our widget:

```
register_sidebar_widget('Aside', 'widget_aside_render');
register_widget_control('Aside', 'widget_aside_admin', 350, 200);
```

So WordPress will execute the `widget_aside_admin()` function and the `widget_aside_render()` function in the admin state and the display state, respectively. Let us first discuss the admin state.

In this widget, we need to store the title of our widget and the note that is supplied by the users. The `update_option()` function will help us to achieve this. This function will store an array as a serialized object in the WordPress database. When you need to restore that data use the `get_option()` function.

In the admin state (that is in the `widget_aside_admin()` function) of our widget, we first check whether anyone has posted any update information . If so, we will store the data in the database. Later, we will restore the information and display it in two input boxes. While rendering the admin panel, ensure that you do not use any HTML `<form>` element, because WordPress already displays the information in an HTML form.

In the display state, there is nothing much to do; we just retrieve the information and display it.

While rendering data in the display state, always echo the `$before_widget` variable first, then the `$before_title` variable, and then your content. Finally, use the `$after_title` variable and the `$after_widget` variable. This is the convention suggested by Automattic to maintain backward compatibility with some themes.

Essential Rules

While developing widgets, please consider the following factors and always try to follow them:

- Carefully choose the name of your widget so that it does not coincide with the name of an already existing one.
- Carefully choose the function name inside your widget. Best practice is to use the namespace format while naming these functions. That is, if your widget

name is **Aside**, add `aside_` as a prefix to all your functions. This will then avoid possible function name duplication. If there are two functions with the same name, it will not work and PHP will generate an error.

- Use the namespace format in the entire form element so as to avoid the possibility of duplication with existing widgets.

- Before creating nice widgets, we would recommend you to read the source code of the original widget plug-in and see how Automattic designed themes. This will increase your widget-creating capability.

Designing Multiple-Instance Widgets

There may be situations when you need multiple instances of your widgets. For example, a user may place several instances of the **Aside** widget in their sidebar. In this section, we will learn how to design widgets with multiple-instance capability.

In widgets with multiple-instance capability, you must handle each widget separately and individually. You must also provide a facility so that users can choose the number of instances of a widget. In the following example, we converted the Aside widget into one having multiple instances:

```
<?
/*
Plugin Name: Aside
Plugin URI: not available
Description: a sample widget for WordPress book
Author: Hasin Hayder
Version: 1.0
Author URI: http://hasin.wordpress.com
*/
function widget_aside_init()
{
  if ( !function_exists('register_sidebar_widget') || !function_
exists('register_widget_control') )
  return;

  add_action('sidebar_admin_page', 'widget_aside_page');
  add_action('sidebar_admin_setup', 'widget_aside_setup');
  widget_aside_setup();
}

function widget_aside_setup()
{
  //echo "accessed";
  if ($_POST['aside_number_submit']=='1')
```

```
  {
    $number_of_asides = $_POST['number_of_asides'];
    update_option("widget_aside_number",$number_of_asides);
  }

  $number_of_asides = get_option("widget_aside_number")+1;

  for ($i=1; $i<$number_of_asides; $i++)
  {
    $name = array('Aside %s', null, $i);
    register_sidebar_widget("Aside {$i}", 'widget_aside_render', $i);
    register_widget_control("Aside {$i}", 'widget_aside_admin', 350,
200,$i);
  }

  for ($i=$number_of_asides; $i<6; $i++)
  {
    register_sidebar_widget("Aside {$i}", '', $i);
    register_widget_control("Aside {$i}", '', 350, 200,$i);
  }
}

function widget_aside_page() {
  $options = $newoptions = get_option('widget_aside');
?>
  <div class="wrap">
    <form method="POST">
      <h2>Aside Widgets</h2>
      <p>How many aside widgets would you like?
      <select name='number_of_asides'>
        <?
          for($i=1; $i<6; $i++)
          echo "<option value={$i}>{$i}</option>";
        ?>
      </select>
      <span class="submit"><input type='hidden' name = 'aside_number_
submit' value='1'><input type="submit" value="save" /></span></p>
    </form>
  </div>
<?php
}

function widget_aside_admin($args)
{
  $widget_id = $args;
  if ($_POST['aside_submit']=='1'){
```

```
    $current_widget_id = $widget_id;//$_POST['aside_id'];
    $options['aside_title'] = $_POST["aside_title{
                                      $current_widget_id}"];
    $options['aside_note'] = $_POST["aside_note{$current_widget_id}"];

  update_option("widget_aside{$current_widget_id}",$options);
  }

  $options = get_option("widget_aside{$widget_id}");
  if (empty($options))
  {
    $title = "Aside";
    $note = "Type your note here";
  }
  else {
    $title = $options['aside_title'];
    $note = $options['aside_note'];
  }
  echo "<div stle='height: 200px'>
      <p style='text-align: left'>
      Title<br/>
      <input type='text' name='aside_title{$widget_id}'
                                    value='{$title}'><br/>
      Note<br/>
      <textarea rows='5' cols='40' name='aside_note{
                      $widget_id}'>{$note}</textarea><br/></p>
      <input type='hidden' name='aside_submit' value='1'>
      <input type='hidden' name='aside_id' value='{$widget_id}'>
      </div>";
}

function widget_aside_render($args,$id)
{
  extract($args);
  $widget_id = $id;
  $options = get_option("widget_aside{$widget_id}");
  if (empty($options))
  {
    $title = "Aside";
    $note = "There is no note currently";
  }
  else {
    $title = $options['aside_title'];
    $note = $options['aside_note'];
  }
```

```
    echo $before_widget;
    echo $before_title;
    echo "<h2>{$title}</h2>";
    echo "<ul><li>{$note}</li></ul>";
    echo $after_title;
    echo $after_widget;
}

add_action('plugins_loaded', 'widget_aside_init');
?>
```

Now if you scroll down the **Sidebar Widgets** page, you will find that you can specify the number of instances of the Aside widget from a drop-down combo box.

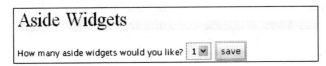

The above portion is rendered by the `widget_aside_page()` function. If you take a look at the code, you will find that the `widget_aside_page()` function executes by hooking the `sidebar_admin_page` action in the format `add_action('sidebar_admin_page', 'widget_aside_page')`.

The following form is managed using the `widget_aside_setup()` function by hooking the `sidebar_admin_setup` action in the format `add_action('sidebar_admin_setup', 'widget_aside_setup')`.

Sidebar Arrangement

You can drag and drop widgets into your sidebar below.

Available Widgets	Sidebar I
Archives ≡	Aside 1 ≡
Aside 4 ≡	Aside 2 ≡
Aside 5 ≡	Aside 3 ≡
Calendar ≡	
Categories ≡	
Links	
Meta ≡	
Pages ≡	
RSS 1 ≡	
Recent Comments ≡	

If you take a look at your WordPress blog now, you will find that all the instances of the Aside widget are rendered correctly.

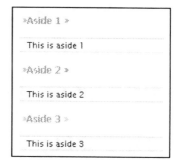

Third-Party Widgets

For some more widgets, you can visit the following URLs:

- `http://widgets.wordpress.com`
- `http://codex.wordpress.org/Plugins/WordPress_Widgets`

Plug-ins

Writing a plug-in is easier than writing a widget. To avoid confusion, a widget is basically a kind of plug-in that executes with the help of the widget plug-in developed by Automattic. In this section, we will understand how plug-ins function in WordPress and how we can develop one on our own.

Plug-ins are simple PHP functions that are invoked at some specific event. Plug-in developers specify those events and ping the WordPress engine to register their plug-in for running at those events. These events are called **hooks**. WordPress has many hooks inside it and those are documented in Codex, the main documentation repository. By intercepting those hooks, you can simply do magic with WordPress. If you are not sure what you can do, take a look at the Tiger Admin panel, which is a replacement of the default WordPress administration panel.

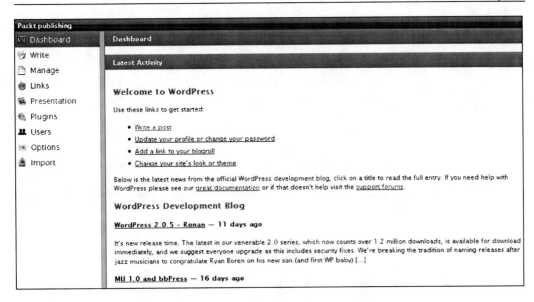

Let us develop a simple plug-in and we will learn through that.

Plug-in: RSS Processor

The RSS processor is a simple plug-in that fetches RSS feeds from a remote site and displays the feed title along with the feed URL. Users will be able to fetch as many RSS feed URLs as they want in each single post and page.

If a user adds the RSS URL in the following format, then only this plug-in will work. The user can also specify how many feeds they want to display through this URL. The format also specifies that the visitors will see the latest five posts from the phpExperts Yahoo group.

```
{rss uri='http://groups.yahoo.com/group/phpexperts/rss' limit='5'}
```

In this plug-in, we are going to use LastRSS, which is an RSS-processing class developed in PHP. You can download the class from http://lastrss.webdot.cz.

```
<?
/*
Plugin Name: RSS Processor
Plugin URI: http://hasin.phpxperts.com/
Description: A plug-in that Fetch RSS feeds and parse to show it, You
can use it in any post of any page
Author: Hasin Hayder
Version: 2.0
Author URI: http://hasin.wordpress.com
```

```
Feature: now supports multi rss source in single post or page.
*/
?>
<?

add_filter('the_content', 'rss_parse');

/**
rss_parse
this function search the content for {rss} tag and then parsse it

sample formats of the {rss} tag
  1. {rss uri=http://rss.groups.yahoo.com/group/phpexperts/
                                                    rss count=5}

there are 2 attribute in this {rss} tag which we look for
  1. uri = rss feed location
  2. limit = how many feed to show

@param string $content the content of the post
@return none
*/
function rss_parse($content)
{
  $rss = new lastRSS();

  $pattern = "~{rss\s*uri=(.*)\s*limit=(.*)}~iU";

  preg_match_all($pattern, $content, $matches);
  $rsses =0;
  while ($rsses<count($matches[0]))
  {
    //initialize the content buffer
    $p_content = "";
    //get the rss uri
    $uri = $matches[1][$rsses];
    //get how many rss feed to show on page
    $count = $matches[2][$rsses];

    //initialize the counter
    if (empty($count)) $count = 10;

    //parse it
    $rss_content = $rss->Get($uri);
    //get all the items
    $items = $rss_content['items'];
```

```
    //parse the items
    $i=0;
    while($i<$count)
    {
        $p_content .= "<div id='rss_item'><strong><a href='{$items[$i]['
link']}'>".$items[$i]['title']."</a></strong><br/>";
        $p_content .= "".$items[$i]['description']."</div><br/><br/>";

        $i++;

    }

    $content = str_replace($matches[0][$rsses], $p_content, $content);
    $rsses +=1;
    }
    return $content;
}
?>
```

Let us use this plug-in and make a sample post in our blog. Prior to that, remember to activate the plug-in.

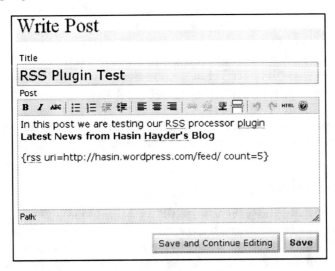

Now if you access the blog, you will see that the remote content has been fetched and displayed properly.

RSS Plugin Test

August 23, 2006 at 2:15 am · Filed under Uncategorized · Edit

In this post we are testing our RSS processor plugin

Latest News from Hasin Hayder's Blog

Creating Thumbnail of WebPages using WebThumb API

Joshua Eichorn, the author of "Understanding AJAX" and a renowned php developer recently released WebThumb, a site to create thumbnails of web pages. The whole system is developed in c and it uses Mozilla engine to render the webpage into images. Shortly after publishing WebThumb, he released a set of API so that developers can [...]

Generate Thumbnail of Any Webpage using PHP

Joshua Eichorn recently released a fantastic service for creating thumbnail of webpages at runtime. The service is named as "WebThumb". Later he relesed some API for developers to incorporate the service using a API-Key. The API-Key is available after registering at the site. Today I made a PHP Wrapper of his WebThumb API using [...]

Hooks

Hooks are the main means through which plug-ins work. Hooks are a kind of event in the WordPress execution process that you can intercept to inject a function to work in that event. There are two types of hooks, namely action hooks and filter hooks. Action hooks take place when some action occurs, for example when someone makes a post, an action hook will be triggered. Action hooks won't ask for any information to be returned to WordPress. They only specify that an action has occurred. Filter hooks are similar, but they return information back to WordPress. For example, WordPress will pass the content of a post to your plug-in and you may change it, modify it, and then return the content to WordPress.

Understanding Hooks

The preceding RSS plug-in works using a filter hook. It intercepts at the `the_content` hook, which returns the content of the post. Let us create another plug-in that will filter blacklisted words in the user-defined list and replace them with *****. We will hook the `pre_comment_content` filter that occurs just before saving the content of the comment in the database. The following code achieves this functionality:

```
<?
/*
Plugin Name: Blacklisted Words Remover
Plugin URI: NA
Description: A sample plug-in for WordPress book
```

```
Author: Hasin Hayder
Version: 1.0
Author URI: http://hasin.phpxperts.com
*/
?>
<?

add_filter('pre_comment_content', 'blacklist_process');

function blacklist_process($content
{
  $blacklist = array("sample1", "sample2", "sample3", "sample4");
  foreach($blacklist as $bword)
  {
    $content = str_replace($bword, "******", $content);
  }
  return $content;
}

?>
```

So when someone makes a comment as shown in the following screenshot, the output will be like the next screenshot shown overleaf.

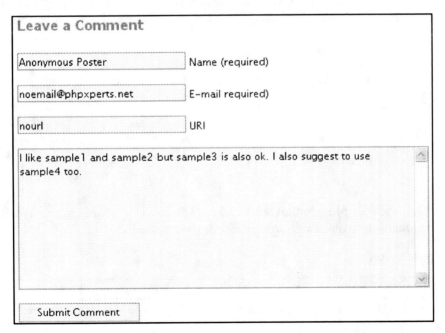

After posting this comment, take a look at the blog:

> Anonymous Poster said,
> September 10, 2006 @ 1:00 am
>
> I like ****** and ****** but ****** is also ok. I also suggest to use ****** too.

I hope you now understand how these plug-ins work with action and filter hooks.

Automated Installation of Plug-ins with DB Access

If your plug-in has to access the database, there are several choices. You may supply the SQL statements necessary to create tables according to the requirement of your plug-in. The blog admin will then manually execute those SQL statements to make your plug-in work. However, if you do this, your blog admin may not be experienced enough to manage these database operations. So you have to think of an alternative idea.

Fortunately, in WordPress plug-ins can automate the whole process. That is, when someone activates your plug-in, you can capture that event and check whether the necessary tables exist in the database. If not, you will execute the necessary SQL statements to create the required tables. The entire process is transparent and your users need not bother about the installation.

In order to check the event when someone activates a plug-in, let us use the following code:

```
if (isset($_GET['activate']) && $_GET['activate'] == 'true') {
  //Now you are in the activation event. Do the database operation
    //here

}
```

Let us create a simple plug-in that stores all the searched keywords in our WordPress blog into a database table. Table structure will be as follows:

table wp_searchedwords:

Field	Type	Null	Key	Default	Extra
id	int(11)	YES	PRI	NULL	auto_increment
word	varchar(255)			NULL	

When someone conducts a search, WordPress receives a GET request where the variable name is s; so the $_GET['s'] parameter describes the searched for words. To process any $_GET or $_POST parameter, we should hook the init action hook. Let us take a look at the following plug-in code:

```
<?
/*
Plugin Name: Searched Words
Plugin URI: NA
Description: A sample plug-in for WordPress book
Author: Hasin Hayder
Version: 1.0
Author URI: http://hasin.phpxperts.com


*/
?>
<?

add_filter('init', 'searchedwords_init');
add_action("admin_menu","admin_menu");

function searchedwords_init($content)
{
  if (isset($_GET['activate']) && $_GET['activate'] == 'true') {
    global $wpdb;

    $result = mysql_list_tables(DB_NAME);
    $current_tables = array();
    while ($row = mysql_fetch_row($result)) {
      $current_tables[] = $row[0];
    }
    if (!in_array("wp_searchedwords", $current_tables))
    {
      $result = mysql_query(
                        "CREATE TABLE`wp_searchedwords
                                    (id INT NOT NULL
                                    AUTO_INCREMENT
                                    PRIMARY KEY,
                                    word VARCHAR(255)
                                    )");

    }
  }

  if (!empty($_GET['s']))
  {
```

```
    $current_searched_words = explode(" ",urldecode($_GET['s']));
    foreach ($current_searched_words as $word)
    {
      mysql_query("insert into wp_searchedwords values(null,
'{$word}')");
    }
  }
}

function admin()
{
  echo "<div class='wrap'>";
  $result = mysql_query("select count(word) as occurance, word from
wp_searchedwords group by word order by occurance DESC");
  echo "<h2>Top Searched Words</h2>";
  if (mysql_num_rows($result)>0)
  {
    while ($row = mysql_fetch_row($result))
    {
      echo "People searched for <b>{$row[1]}</b> for {$row[0]}
  time(s)<br/>";
    }
  }
  else {
    echo "<h3>Sorry - No searchword found</h3>";
  }

  echo "</div>";
}

function admin_menu()
{
  if (function_exists('add_submenu_page')) {
    add_submenu_page('index.php', "Searched Keywords", "Searched
Keywords", 1, 'searchedwords.plugin.php', 'admin');
  }
}
?>
```

Save this plug-in as searchedwords.plugin.php in the plug-in folder of WordPress and activate it from the **Plugins** menu. As soon as you activate the plug-in, it creates a wp_searchedwords table in your WordPress blog database as follows:

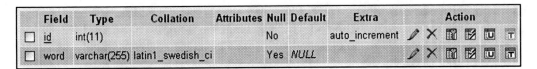

	Field	Type	Collation	Attributes	Null	Default	Extra	Action
☐	id	int(11)			No		auto_increment	
☐	word	varchar(255)	latin1_swedish_ci		Yes	*NULL*		

Moreover, as soon as you activate the plug-in, go to the **Dashboard** to find an extra menu called **Searched Keywords**.

Now if you click on this **Searched Keywords** menu for the first time, you will find the following screen:

The preceding screen shows that no keywords are found because this is our first time. Since no one searched for anything in our blog, the table is empty. Now let us search for something in our blog from the search box in the sidebar and come back to this **Searched Keywords** page. Now you will see the actual result.

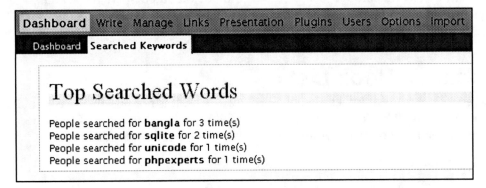

In this plug-in, we also introduced how to add admin pages inside the WordPress admin panel. Let us analyze the code and see what has actually happened.

Dissecting the Code

Firstly, we hooked the `init` action hook to process the request parameters and then we hooked the `admin_menu` hook to add our admin page.

```
add_filter('init', 'searchedwords_init');
add_action("admin_menu","admin_menu");
```

Thereafter, WordPress will access the `searchedwords_init` function inside our plug-in. In this function, we first check if the `wp_searchedwords` table exists in the WordPress database. If not, we will create this table.

We then check if there are any search requests. If available, we just store them in the database.

To add the admin page, we used the `admin_menu()` function. In this function, we added a function in the index page (dashboard).

```
add_submenu_page('index.php',  "Searched Keywords",  "Searched
Keywords", 1, 'searchedwords.plugin.php', 'admin');
```

The format of this function is as follows:

```
function add_submenu_page($parent, $page_title, $menu_title, $access_
level, $file, $function = '')
```

So our code just adds an admin menu called **Searched Keywords** under the **Dashboard** section that will access the `admin()` function of `searchedwords.plugin.php`, which is our plug-in file.

In the `admin()` function, we just analyze our database and display the searched keywords in ascending order. This function will be accessed each time anyone clicks on **Searched Keywords** from the admin panel.

Common Hook List

There are hundreds of hooks available in WordPress. It is not possible to cover all of them in this small book. However, you can visit the online reference of these hooks for further study. For most common hooks browse the following URLs:

- Plug-in API in Codex (http://codex.wordpress.org/Plugin_API)
- WordPress 2.x action hooks list (http://blog.taragana.com/index.php/archive/wordpress-2x-hooks-for-action-comprehensive-list-for-plugin-and-theme-developers/)

- WordPress 2.x filter hooks list (`http://blog.taragana.com/index.php/archive/wordpress-2x-filters-comprehensive-list-for-plugin-and-theme-developers/`)

- WordPress hook list (`http://wphooks.flatearth.org/`)

- Skippy's hook list (`http://codex.wordpress.org/User:Skippy`)

These URLs deliver the most comprehensive list of WordPress hooks.

Summary

Extending an existing system is always an interesting and challenging job. You have to care about the existing code base and structure and extend it in such a way that the design does not collapse after merging those extensions. This chapter discusses extending WordPress in detail by developing plug-ins and widgets. This chapter also shows us how to design widgets with multiple-instance support.

Extending WordPress is like a never-ending adventure. These days many services are published with an extremely simple set of APIs and we can integrate many of those into our WordPress blog. So reading this chapter will help you start this amazing journey by yourself.

10

Administrator's Reference

While blogging, various troubles may arise. You should have the proper knowledge to troubleshoot these problems. Moreover, having some advanced experience with WordPress will save your time in need. This chapter will give you an advanced view of WordPress, help you to troubleshoot problems, and give you a closer look at the ins and outs of WordPress.

System Requirements

Although WordPress usually works pretty well with **LAMP** and **WAMP** (LAMP stands for Linux-Apache-MySQL-PHP, and WAMP stands for Windows-Apache-MySQL-PHP), there are several issues with both these platforms. We will have a closer look at these issues in this section.

WordPress requires a web server that can run PHP with the support of MySQL to function properly. The best web servers that work with PHP are Apache, IIS, and LiteSpeed. Let us take a look at the requirements here:

Web Server: Apache, LiteSpeed, or IIS
(`http://httpd.apache.org/`, `http://litespeedtech.com/`, `http://www.iis.net/`)

PHP: Version 4.2 or later

MySQL: 3.23.23 or greater

If you want to have permalinks with custom URLs enabled in your blog, you must have Apache web server with `mod_rewrite` enabled in your server. If `mod_rewrite` is not available, the permalink URL may not look so friendly. However, in most cases Apache `mod_rewrite` is installed on web hosting accounts. You may mail to your system administrator if you don't have it installed on your account.

A Closer Look at the Installation

In Chapter 2, we discussed how you can install WordPress locally as well as remotely. We also saw how to install WordPress from cPanels. In this section, we will have a closer look at the other important topics of installation like upgrading WordPress, migrating WordPress data from one server to another, installing WordPress for a multi-user environment, setting file permissions, uninstalling WordPress, different kinds of troubleshooting during these processes, and finally backing up files and database of WordPress.

Upgrading WordPress

You may have an older version of WordPress installed on your machine like 1.5.x or even 1.2.x, and may already have a stable blog running. So choosing a new installation will not be a wise decision in these cases. The best option is upgrading your old WordPress installation to the new version, without losing your data and other files. Let us see how we can upgrade WordPress.

To upgrade, you have to follow the following steps. The process would also be similar if you want to upgrade from the 2.x version to a higher one.

Step 1: Back Up your Database

Before upgrading WordPress, we must back up our existing database. There is no assurance that nothing will go wrong. Thus, we should better avoid the risk of losing our database.

This is a most important step that you must do with proper attention. You can use any MySQL front-end like MySQL-front, phpMyAdmin, or even MySQL client for backing up your database. Please refer to the *Backups* section later in this chapter to know how to back up your WordPress database.

Step 2: Back Up your WordPress Files

Before proceeding further, you must perform one more backup. You must back up all the WordPress files including plug-ins, themes, and .htaccess files. You can do this by logging into your WordPress directory using an FTP client. We will discuss these in details later in this chapter in the *Backing Up WordPress Files* section.

Step 3: Verifying the Backups

After performing the backups, the major step is to verify whether the backed up files are OK and usable. If they were interrupted while downloading, they may not be usable in many cases. In that case, there is a great risk of losing all your data.

So always verify your backup files. Remember not to skip this step.

Step 4: Deactivate All Your Plug-ins

The plug-ins that are working with the current installation of WordPress on your machine may not work with the upgraded installation of WordPress. If a plug-in breaks, your WordPress installation will not work as well. So before upgrading WordPress, you must deactivate all the active plug-ins.

To deactivate plug-ins, log into your WordPress administration panel and click on the **Plugins** menu. If you are using WordPress 1.5.x, you will see a screen similar to the following:

Plugin Management

Plugins are files you usually download separately from WordPress that add functionality. To install a plugin you generally just need to put the plugin file into your wp-content/plugins directory. Once a plugin is installed, you may activate it or deactivate it here. If something goes wrong with a plugin and you can't use WordPress, delete that plugin from the wp-content/plugins directory and it will be automatically deactivated.

Plugin	Version	Author	Description	Action
Hello Dolly	1.0	Matt Mullenweg	This is not just a plugin, it symbolizes the hope and enthusiasm of an entire generation summed up in two words sung most famously by Louis Armstrong. Hello, Dolly. This is, by the way, the world's first official WordPress plugin. When enabled you will randomly see a lyric from Hello, Dolly in the upper right of your admin screen on every page.	Deactivate
Markdown	1.0.1	Michel Fortin	Markdown syntax allows you to write using an easy-to-read, easy-to-write plain text format. Based on the original Perl version by John Gruber. More...	Deactivate
RSS Processor	2.0	Hasin Hayder	A plugin that aggregates RSS and parse to show it, You can use it in any post of any page	Activate

On the right side of this page, you can deactivate all the active plug-ins by clicking on the **Deactivate** links.

Step 5: Download and Extract WordPress

Now download the WordPress ZIP file onto your machine. If you have shell access, then you can also download WordPress in the web directory.

After downloading WordPress, extract all the files in a new folder named **WordPress**. If you are using Windows, then you can right-click on the ZIP file and extract using WinZip/WinRar software. If you are using *nix, then unzip all the files using the gunzip command.

```
gunzip -c wordpressfilename.zip | tar -xf -
```

If you downloaded tarballs, you can use the following command:

```
using: tar -xzvf latest.tar.gz
```

Step 6: Delete Old Files

Now delete all the files of your previous WordPress installation except the following listed files and directories. You can use any FTP client for deleting these files. You can also use shell commands. If you don't have an FTP client, you can use the best web-based FTP program: Net2FTP.

- `wp-config.php` file
- `wp-content` folder
- `wp-images` folder
- If you used a specific language pack, then don't delete the `wp-includes/languages/` folder
- If you used custom `mod_rewrite` or permalinks, then don't delete the `.htaccess` files
- `wp-content/plugins` folder, if you used custom plug-ins
- `wp-content/themes` folder, if you had custom themes

If you have shell access, then use the following commands to delete the unnecessary files. The command sequences have been taken directly from WordPress **Help**. These commands place the necessary files inside a folder named **backup** in the current directory.

- `mkdir backup`
- `cp wp-config.php .htaccess wp-layout.css index.php wp-comments.php wp-comments-popup.php backup`
- `cp -R wp-content backup`
- `rm wp*.php wp-layout.css .htaccess`
- `rm -rf wp-admin wp-images wp-includes`
- `cp backup/wp-config.php`

The third command, `cp -R wp-content backup`, copies the whole **wp-content** folder recursively inside the **backup** folder. So you can always restore any necessary files from this backup folder.

Log into your WordPress hosting account from any FTP client (for example, Filezilla). You will see something like this:

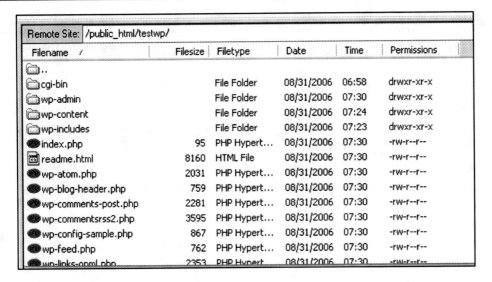

Now right-click on the folder that you wish to delete, for example **wp-admin**, and hit the *Delete* key. It will be deleted instantly.

Deleting Folders Using Net2FTP

Net2FTP is one of the best web-based FTP programs and is an open-source script developed using PHP. The official Net2FTP site hosts this script. So you can perform FTP operation using this site at no cost at all.

To start the FTP operation, point your browser to `http://www.net2ftp.com`. You will find a login panel on the left-hand side.

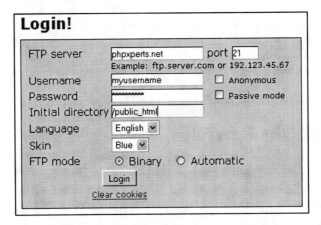

Log into your WordPress FTP account using your username and password. If your login is successful, you will see something like the following page:

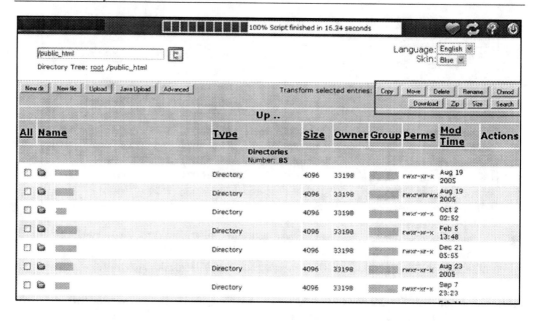

At the upper-right corner, which is outlined, you will find the necessary buttons for file manipulation. Please note that there is a checkbox on the left-hand side of every folder. Clicking on the folder named **wordpress**, you will get into the WordPress folder immediately. Now, to delete the **wp-admin** folder, check the checkbox just beside the **wp—admin** folder. Click on the **Delete** button from the upper-right portion of this page. You will be redirected to a page like the following:

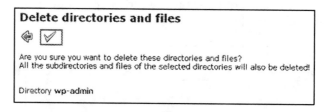

Finally, click on the button outlined.

Step 7: Upload the New Files

Connect to your WordPress host directory using your FTP client or Net2FTP and then upload the new files you extracted in *Step 5*. Using Net2FTP, you can directly upload the ZIP file or tarball, and Net2FTP will extract it immediately after uploading it to the current directory. You can upload all the files using any FTP client. If you have shell access, you can even upload the ZIP file or tarball and then extract it using shell commands as shown in *Step 5*.

Just remember that when you upload using Net2FTP, some files in your old WordPress installation will be overwritten by some of the new ones and that is recommended. If you use any FTP client, allow it to overwrite.

Step 8: Run the WordPress Upgrade Program

After completing the preceding seven steps, now it's finally time to run the upgrade script. Point your browser to `http://your_wordpress_directory/wp-admin/upgrade.php`.

This file upgrades you from any previous version of WordPress to the latest. It may take a while though, so be patient.

Upgrade WordPress »

Click on the **Upgrade WordPress** link.

Step 1

There's actually only one step. So if you see this, you're done. Have fun!

That's it, you are done. Now you can log in using your old username and password. Upgrading WordPress is an absolutely hassle-free process.

Step 9: Update Permalinks and .htaccess

If you were using permalink settings in your previous installation, please log into your upgraded WordPress as the administrator and update the well formatted permalink structure as in the previous installation. In this case, you have to update the `.htaccess` file of the current installation to the version that your old WordPress installation used.

Step 10: Install Updated Plug-ins and Themes

Make a list of your plug-ins that were running with the previous version of WordPress. The WordPress community makes a comprehensive list of plug-ins that are compatible with an upgraded version. Visit the URL and download all the up-to-date versions of your plug-ins (`http://codex.wordpress.org/User:Matt/2.0_Plugin_Compatibility`).

Step 11: Reactivate Plug-ins

If everything runs OK and completed successfully, it's time to reactivate plug-ins. You can do it by logging in as the administrator, and then going to the plug-ins menu. It is recommended to activate plug-ins one by one and see whether it still works correctly or not. If any problem occurs, consider that plug-in as not compatible with this upgraded version of WordPress.

Migrating WordPress

Sometimes you may have to move from one server to another. If it was not possible to move your blog, all your blogging efforts would be worthless. This migration could be of two types:

- Migration within your server, that is from one directory to another directory
- Migration to another server

Fortunately, WordPress provides ways to migrate your blog. Here we discuss both cases of migration.

Migrating within the Same Site

For migrating within the same site, follow these steps:

- Create the directory where you want to move this installation
- Log into your old blog as administrator
- Select the **Options** menu, and then select the **General** sub-menu. You will get the following screen:

General Options

Weblog title:	My First Blog
Tagline:	Just another WordPress weblog
	In a few words, explain what this weblog is about.
WordPress address (URI):	http://phpxperts.net/wordpress
Blog address (URI):	http://phpxperts.net/wordpress
	If you want your blog homepage to be different than the directory you installed WordPress in, enter that address here.

Now let us assume that we are moving WordPress from this **wordpress** folder to the **wp2** folder.

1. Change the WordPress address to the new location, for example `http://phpxperts.net/wp2`.

2. Change the blog address URI to the new location, for example `http://phpxperts.net/wp2`.

3. Save the options by clicking the **Update Options** button.

4. Log out from your admin panel.

5. Copy your files to the new location.

6. Now visit the new location.

Migrating from One Server to Another

For migrating WordPress from one server to another, follow these steps:

1. Make a back up of your existing database; we have to edit this SQL file later.

2. Back up all files in your WordPress folder to a back up folder.

3. Open the `wp-config.php` file from your existing WordPress directory.

```php
<?php
// ** MySQL settings ** //
define('DB_NAME', 'wp');          // The name of the database
define('DB_USER', 'root');         // Your MySQL username
define('DB_PASSWORD', 'root');  // ...and password
define('DB_HOST', 'localhost');    // 90% chance you
won't need to change this value
```

Edit the third, fourth, fifth, and sixth lines according to the database name, database username, database password, and the hostname of your new server. Mostly, you don't need to change the hostname.

4. Open the SQL file that you created while backing up the WordPress database. Replace all instances of your old WordPress URL with the new one. For example, if your existing WordPress URL is `http://olddomain/wordpress` and your new URL is `http://newdomain/wordpress`, then replace all instances of `http://olddomain/wordpress` inside your SQL file with `http://newdomain/wordpress`. You can do this using any text editor. Save this modified version of your SQL file.

5. Upload all your WordPress files from the old installation to the new directory. Don't miss any file. Keep them as is.

6. Now restore the database using the modified version of your SQL file. If you don't know how to restore database from SQL files, read the *Restoring the Database from a Backup* section that comes later in this chapter.

7. Open phpMyAdmin (or connect to the new server's MySQL host using any MySQL client), select the new WordPress database that you just restored, and run the following SQL command:

```
update wp_options set option_value='new_wordpress_URL'
where option_name='siteurl' and option_value='home'
```

You can run SQL by clicking on the **SQL** tab in the top-right pane. A practical example could be something like this:

```
update wp_options set option_value='http://newdomain/wordpress'
where option_name='siteurl' and option_value='home'
```

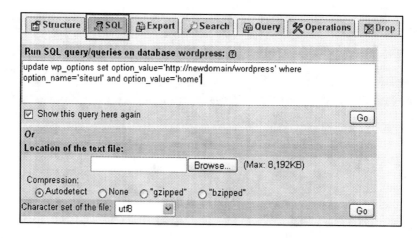

8. Change the permissions of your **wp-content** folder to `rwxrwxrwx 777` for file upload facility.

9. You have to find out the absolute path of your WordPress folder in the server. You can do this by running a PHP file inside your WordPress **wp-content** folder. The code of this PHP file is: `<? echo getcwd();?>`. Now execute this file using your browser. For example, if the output is something like `home\user\phpxperts\htdocs\wordpress`, then run the following SQL command in phpMyAdmin:

```
update wp_options set option_value= 'home\user\phpxperts\htdocs\
wordpress' where option_name= 'fileupload_realpath'
```

10. Now open your `.htaccess` file and see if it is blank or not. If blank, then you can copy your old `.htaccess` file here.

11. Browse the new URL of your migrated WordPress.

Multiple Installations

A multi-user environment is a WordPress hosting environment where a lot of users can register and blog separately. Each of them will get their own blog. All blogs run independently of one another. If you set up a multi-user environment, then you can host blogs for a lot of users.

There are different techniques to set up a multi-user environment for WordPress:

- Using different databases
- Using a single database
- Using third-party solutions

Using different databases, you can set up as many blogs as you want. This is just normally installing WordPress under the same domain by modifying the wp-config.php file. However, this technique depends upon your hosting facilities. If you have limited database options, then it is not the best solution for you.

Using single database, you can install as many WordPress blogs as you want. You can do this by just changing the table prefix in the wp-config.php file.

```
1   <?php
2   // ** MySQL settings ** //
3   define('DB_NAME', 'wp');        // The name of the database
4   define('DB_USER', 'root');      // Your MySQL username
5   define('DB_PASSWORD', 'root');  // ...and password
6   define('DB_HOST', 'localhost');   // 99% chance you
    won't need to change this value
7
8   // You can have multiple installations in one database
    if you give each a unique prefix
9   $table_prefix = 'wp_';  // Only numbers, letters, and
    underscores please!
```

The preceding screenshot shows a typical `wp-config.php` file. You can have many WordPress installations under the same database by changing the ninth line. Make the `$table_prefix` different for different users. That's it.

The final solution for setting up a multi-user environment is using third-party solutions. WordPress community develops a different version of WordPress just for setting up a multi-user blogging environment. This is called **WordPress MU**. WordPress MU is derived from the words **WordPress** multi-user.

WordPress MU

WordPress MU is a different product, which is maintained and developed separately. This version of WordPress is not supported officially and not maintained for general users. So the development process is a bit slow. Moreover, there are some complexities in maintaining and installing WordPress MU. So it is not a WordPress version for all bloggers. If you are an advanced user, you can take up the challenge.

WordPress MU is the ultimate solution for a multi-user environment. Although, it offers limited functionality and limited themes and plug-ins, WordPress MU offers the ability to manage each blog separately and securely. The famous multi-user blog hosts WordPress.com, edublogs.org, PRblogs.org, Bloggoing.com, Blogsome.com, and WeblogUP.com are all powered by WordPress MU.

Benefits of Using WordPress MU

There are several benefits of using WordPress MU. If you are a general blogger, then the benefits for you are:

- You can set up your own blog without any hassle or knowing anything. You don't even have to edit any configuration files. Just register your username and start blogging instantly.
- Built-in comment spam protection.
- Ability to use different pre-added themes.
- You will get support from a big community of WordPress MU users.

System Requirements for WordPress MU

WordPress MU requires everything that is required by WordPress itself. Besides, WordPress MU requires something more to run. Let us take a look at the requirements:

Web Server: Apache or Lightship or IIS

PHP: Version 4.2 or later

MySQL: 3.23.23 or greater

Smarty template engine, which is included with WordPress MU by default.

Apache `mod_rewrite`

Apache Symlinks. Wordpress MU developers have said that they will remove the necessity for this package in later versions.

Installing WordPress MU

Download the WordPress MU ZIP file from the website at `http://mu.wordpress.org`. WordPress MU is still released as an unstable version and is under serious development. So the ZIP archive is named as `wpmu-unstable.zip`. Extract all the files from this archive to your WordPress directory using any FTP client.

Create a MySQL database for installing WordPress MU. Let us assume it is `wpmu`.

Point your browser to the WordPress MU URL. When the page comes for the first time, you will see that it prompts for a new installation.

On the lower portion of this page, you will see a form to input necessary database parameters. Please input all necessary parameters. Ensure that the permission to your `wp-config.php` file is writable or is set to `766` for your user account. Finally, click on **Submit**.

Below you should enter your database connection details. If you're not sure about these, contact your host.

Database Name	wordpress	The name of the database you want to run WP in.
User Name	username	Your MySQL username
Password	password	...and MySQL password.
Database Host	localhost	99% chance you won't need to change this value.
Table Prefix	wp_	If you want to run multiple WordPress installations in a single database, change this.

Submit

Please input your blog title. This is the main WordPress MU account. After inserting the necessary data, please click **Submit** for the final step.

WordPressμ

Welcome to WordPress MU, the Multi User Weblog System built on WordPress.

Creating Database Config File: DONE

To finish setting up your blog, please fill in the folling form and click "Submit".

Weblog Title	My new Blog	What would you like to call your weblog?
Email		Your email address.

Submit

You will be sent an email with your password and login links and details.

That's it! Installation of WordPress MU is complete. The password and all the necessary information will be sent to your email account that you provided in the second step.

WordPressμ

Welcome to WordPress MU, the Multi User Weblog System built on WordPress.

Well Done! Your blog has been set up and you have been sent details of your login and password in an email.

You may view your new blog by visiting http://localhost/wpMU/!

After installing, you can customize the look of your WordPress MU page by editing wordpressmu_path/wp-content/themese/home/home.php.

Installing Other People's Blogs in WordPress MU

You have just finished installing the WordPress multi-user version. Other people may now want to set up their blogs in WordPress MU. When they visit your WordPress MU page, they will see the following screen:

My Multiuser Blog
Just another weblog

Localhost

This is a WordPress Mu powered site.

You can:

- Login
- Create a new blog
- Edit this file at wp-content/themes/home/home.php with your favourite text editor and customize this screen.

Please note that there are two links for logging into WPMU admin panel. One link is the usual login link, and another is to set up a new blog. When visitors click on this, they can set up their own blogs. Let us take a look at this page.

Their blog is just one step away. Click on the **Sign up** button and it's done! They will get their administration information at the email address they provided. If the blog setup is successful, they will be redirected to the next page:

So setting up multiple blogs using WordPress MU is very easy.

Uninstalling WordPress

If you want to uninstall WordPress from your machine, it's an easy and hassle-free process. Follow these steps to uninstall WordPress from your machine:

- Make a back up for your database.
- Make a back up of your WordPress files, if you may ever want to start from your old blog.

- Delete the WordPress directory. If you have shell access and proper privilege, apply this shell command in your shell:

  rm -rf your_wordpress_directory

- Log into MySQL using phpMyAdmin or any MySQL client. If you have privilege to delete the database, then apply the following SQL command for deleting your WordPress database: DROP DATABASE your_wordpress_database.

In phpMyAdmin, you may not have the privilege to execute the DROP DATABASE statement. In that case, select your database and click on the **Drop** link at the upper-right corner of the right pane as shown in the following screenshot:

Export	Search	Query	Operations	Drop

Action						Records	Type	Collation
					X	1	MyISAM	latin1_swedish_ci
					X	1	MyISAM	latin1_swedish_ci
					X	1	MyISAM	latin1_swedish_ci

If you don't have proper privilege to delete your database or you installed WordPress in a common database that you use for other purposes also, then delete the following tables. Here I assume that your tables are prefixed by wp_:

- wp_categories
- wp_comments
- wp_linkcategories
- wp_links
- wp_options
- wp_post2cat
- wp_postmeta
- wp_posts
- wp_usermeta
- wp_users

You can delete any table using the DROP TABLE SQL command. For example, if you want to delete the wp_categories table, apply the following SQL command:

DROP TABLE wp_categories

Be sure before deleting these files.

Setting File Permissions

To install and maintain WordPress properly, you may need to change permissions to different files and folders in the WordPress directory. If you are using a Windows operating system, then file permission does not matter. However for Linux, permission does matter. If you don't set proper permissions, you may not be able to install WordPress and it will not function properly.

File permissions are settings that indicate who is privileged to do what. That is, in Linux some users may alter the content of a file, some may just read it, or some may not even have read or write access. Besides read/write permissions, there are also "execute" permissions. If a file is an executable file, then this permission indicates who can execute the file. Before setting permissions for WordPress, let's discuss the significance of the following files and folders:

- `/ or root`: This is the root directory that contains all WordPress files and folders. If your WordPress directory resides on `\home\user\hasin\web\htdocs\wp`, then your root directory for WordPress is the `wp` folder. All the files in this directory must be writable only by you.

- `/wp-admin`: This folder contains all the functions and files required for administering WordPress. This folder must be writable by general users, or at least by users who have privileges to upload plug-ins or modify themes.

- `/wp-includes`: This is the place where all WordPress core files reside. This folder must be writable by the owner, which means "you".

- `/wp-content`: This is the folder that contains user files like themes, plug-ins, uploaded images, etc. This must be writable by your user account.

- `/wp-content/themes`: This is the folder that contains themes. If you use the custom theme editor that comes with WordPress, you may set this folder to writable.

- `/wp-content/plugins`: This is the folder that contains plug-ins. This folder may or may not be writable, depending upon the plug-ins you use.

- `/.htaccess`: If you decide to use custom permalinks, this must be writable by your user account. If you allow custom permalinks or formatted URLs managed automatically by WordPress, you must give write permission to this file.

For file permissions at a glance, look at the following chart:

File/Folder	Owner Permission	Group Permission	User Permission	Total
/	rwx	rw	rw	rwxrw-rw-
/.htaccess	rwx	rw	rw	rwxrw-rw-
/wp-admin	rwx	r--	r--	rwxr--r--
/wp-includes	rwx	r--	r--	rwxr--r--
/wp-content	rwx	rwx	rw-	rwxrwxrw-
/wp-content/themes	rwx	rwx	rw-	rwxrwxrw-
/wp-content/plugins	rwx	rw-	rw-	rwxrw-rw-

How to Set Permissions

You can change permissions to files and folders using any FTP client. If you have shell access, you can even apply shell commands for changing file permissions. Let us see how we can change file permissions using the popular web-based FTP script Net2FTP.

After logging into your hosting account using Net2FTP, you can see a button named **Chmod** at the top-right corner. Select the folder by checking the checkbox beside the name of the folder for which you want to change permission and click on that **Chmod** button. The following screen will appear:

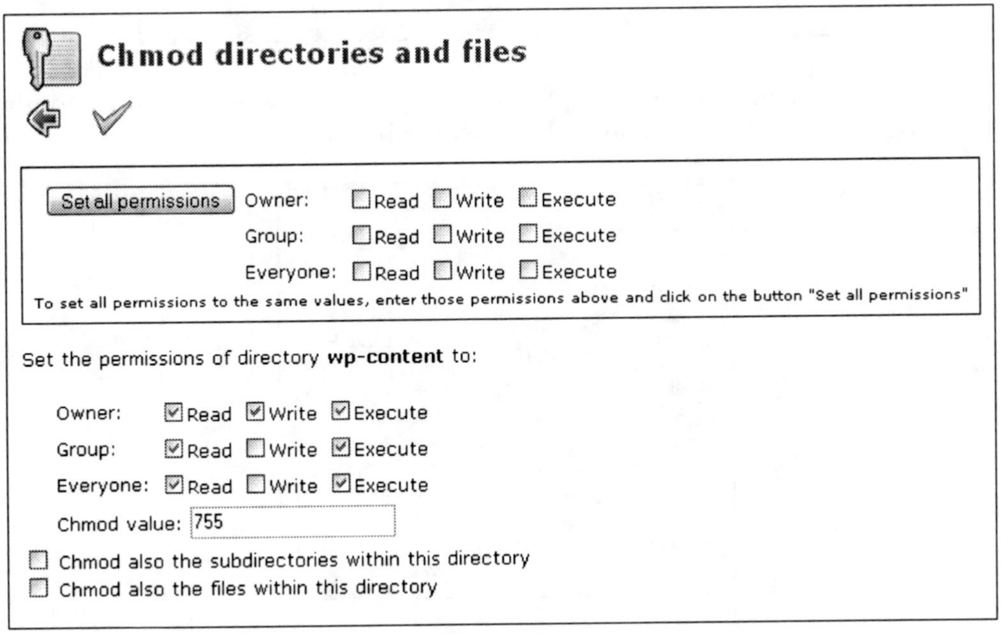

Select the permissions by checking the checkboxes or by writing the value manually (for example, **776** here) and select the green arrow image at the top. You are done!

If you are using shell, change the file permissions with the `chmod` command. For example, the **wp-admin** folder should be set as `rwxr--r--` or `0744`. For example, see the following command:

```
chmod -R wp-admin 0744
```

If you are using an FTP client (for example, Filezilla), you may change permissions as follows.

After logging into your WordPress hosting account, open your WordPress root directory. You will see something like this in your FTP software (I use Filezilla here):

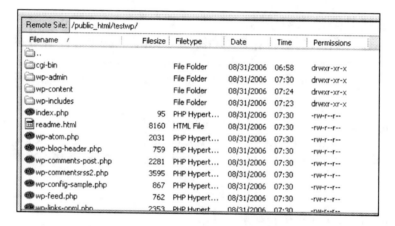

This is the root folder. Now for example, to change the permission for the **wp-admin** folder, right-click on this folder and select **File Attributes**:

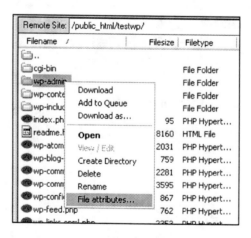

Now a dialog box prompts for file permissions. Check the permissions boxes as shown in the following screenshot:

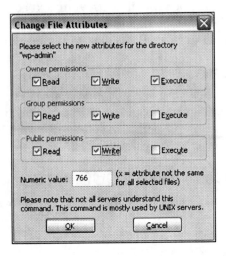

Click **OK**, and you are done. Change permissions for other folders in the same way.

Troubleshooting

In this section, we will discuss the problems that may arise during the installation and execution of WordPress and provide solutions for troubleshooting them.

Troubleshooting during Installation

During installation, different problems may arise. If you are familiar with them, you may sort them quickly, without hunting around for solutions. Most of the problems discussed here have been taken from the WordPress installation FAQs (Frequently Asked Questions) and Troubleshooting FAQs.

Problem: Headers Already Sent

Sometimes, when you point your browser to the blog, you may get an error that displays a **headers already sent** message on your page. The whole page may look scrambled and it will not function.

WordPress uses PHP session functions. If anything is displayed before these session functions, which may even be a blank space, then the session functions will not work properly because your browser has already received all headers and it starts displaying the output. In such circumstances, this error may occur.

You have to figure out where the error has occurred. Most of the time, it is a file that you have edited manually. If you remember, you edited the `wp-config.php` file while installing WordPress. Open the file with your text editor and make sure that there is nothing before the `<?` at the first line and after the `?>` at the last line. Now save this file, upload it to your WordPress directory, and refresh your page again.

Problem: Page Comes with Only PHP Code

This could only happen when your server cannot parse PHP properly. This is a problem of your server configuration; either PHP is not installed on your server or it is not configured to function properly. To solve this problem, contact the system administrator for your server or try installing PHP.

Problem: Cannot Connect MySQL Database

If WordPress cannot connect to the MySQL database, it shows a page like the following screen:

WordPress

Error establishing a database connection

This either means that the username and password information in your `wp-config.php` file is incorrect or we can't contact the database server at `localhost`. This could mean your host's database server is down.

- Are you sure you have the correct username and password?
- Are you sure that you have typed the correct hostname?
- Are you sure that the database server is running?

If you're unsure what these terms mean you should probably contact your host. If you still need help you can always visit the WordPress Support Forums.

To solve this problem, open your `wp-config.php` file and check whether the database parameters are correct. If you are sure that these settings are fine, please check if the MySQL daemon/service is running properly. If MySQL is not running, run this service. If MySQL was running, try restarting the service.

In MySQL version 4.1 and later, password encryption settings have been changed a bit, so PHP cannot connect to some versions of MySQL. If you are sure that your database parameters are fine and MySQL is also running, then connect to MySQL using your MySQL command-line tool and apply these commands:

```
set password = OLD_PASSWORD('your_current_password');
flush privileges;
```

This will use old encryption of passwords so that PHP can connect to MySQL. For example, let's assume my current database password is `root` with new encryption settings. I want to change it to old encryption settings. The following screenshot illustrates this:

```
Enter password: ****
Welcome to the MySQL monitor.  Commands end with ; or \g.
Your MySQL connection id is 11 to server version: 4.1.14-nt-log

Type 'help;' or '\h' for help. Type '\c' to clear the buffer.

mysql> set password = OLD_PASSWORD('root');
Query OK, 0 rows affected (0.00 sec)

mysql> FLUSH PRIVILEGES;
Query OK, 0 rows affected (0.00 sec)

mysql>
```

Basic Troubleshooting

The best place where you can find help for WordPress is its own help system, `http://codex.wordpress.org/Troubleshooting`. No other site is comparable with it. Following are some basic and common problems that you may face while using WordPress.

Problem: Cannot See Posts, All It Says is Search Doesn't Meet Criteria

This could happen because of caching. For example, you have searched once and WordPress stored the search result inside its cache. So every time you visit the page you see the old result. You can solve this problem by clearing the cache and cookies from your browser. For this problem, you may also check `search.php` and `index.php` for errors.

Problem: I Want to Make My Blog Totally Private

If you are running your blog for a personal and private group or for your own official department so that only members of your group can see it, then you would want to secure it with some kind of authentication. WordPress has no built-in facility to do it. All you have to do is modify your `.htaccess` file to enable basic HTTP authentication. For that, you have to create the `htpasswd` file using the `htpasswd` command in Linux. If you are using Windows, then search in Google for `htpasswd.exe` and download it from a reliable location.

Let's create the `htpasswd` file by applying the following command in your command line:

```
htpasswd -cm .htpasswd myusername
```

This `htpasswd` command is a command-line tool available in all Linux distributions by default. Immediately after applying this command, the command-line tool will prompt you for a password; type your password. Please note that an `htpasswd` file containing the encrypted password has been created in the current working directory for user 'username'. Copy that file to your WordPress folder. The `htpasswd` file itself is of no use, until you tell Apache what to do with it. So let us create a `.htaccess` file in your WordPress folder with the following content, which will tell Apache to turn on basic HTTP authentication using that `htpasswd` file:

```
AuthType Basic
AuthName "Restricted Area"
AuthUserFile "absolute_url_of_your_.htpasswd_file"
require valid-user
```

Save this file inside your WordPress directory as `.htaccess`. Now whenever you browse this WordPress URL using your browser, it requires the username and password that you created previously. You must supply the absolute URL of the `htpasswd` file in the `.htaccess` file; it will not work with a relative URL. For example, if your WordPress folder is located inside the `/home/youraccount/ public_html/wordpress` folder, then the location of the `.htpasswd` file should be `/home/youraccount/public_html/wordpress/.htpasswd`.

If you have trouble retrieving this absolute path, then please don't worry. Create a PHP file inside this WordPress folder with the following code:

```
<? phpinfo(); ?>
```

Now run this file. You will see a page with a lot of text. Search for the text `_SERVER["DOCUMENT_ROOT"]`, and you will find the absolute URL of this folder on the right-hand side of it. See the following screenshot:

_SERVER["DOCUMENT_ROOT"]	/home/phpxpert/public_html
_SERVER["HTTP_ACCEPT"]	text/xml,application/xml,application

Problem: I Don't Receive The Emailed Passwords

This problem may happen if your web server has no SMTP server installed, or if the mail function is explicitly disabled. Please contact your system administrator or try installing sendmail (or any other mail server) properly. It should work.

Problem: I Am Getting A Lot of Comment Spam

Please block comment spam by using black-listed words, which we would have discussed in Chapter 4 under the section *Fighting with Comment Spams*.

However, discussing all these problems will not be a wise idea because we need one or two separate chapters only for troubleshooting. So we have discussed only the basic problems. You can get a lot of help from the following URLs. Moreover, you have the huge user community of WordPress to help you. So always use the support forum and Codex.

- `http://codex.wordpress.org/Troubleshooting`
- `http://wordpress.org/support/forum/3`
- `http://codex.wordpress.org/IRC For support in IRC channel`
- `http://codex.wordpress.org/WordPress_Semantics wordpress jargon`
- `http://codex.wordpress.org/WordPress_IRC_Live_Help`

Backups

In the previous sections, we saw the importance of regular backup. In this section, we will see how to back up your files and databases practically using an FTP client and MySQL client.

Backing Up WordPress Files

Firstly, let us back up the WordPress files using the web-based FTP clients Net2FTP and Filezilla.

Backing Up Files Using Net2FTP

After logging into your WordPress hosting account using Net2FTP, you will see something like the following:

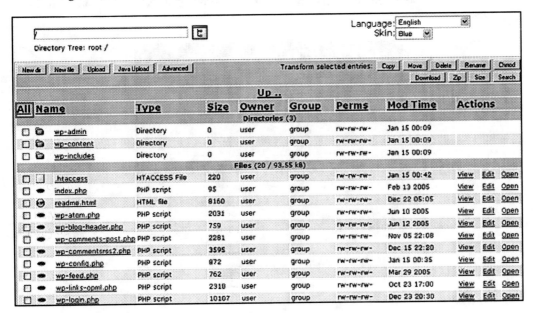

Now click on the **All** link outlined. All files will be selected as follows:

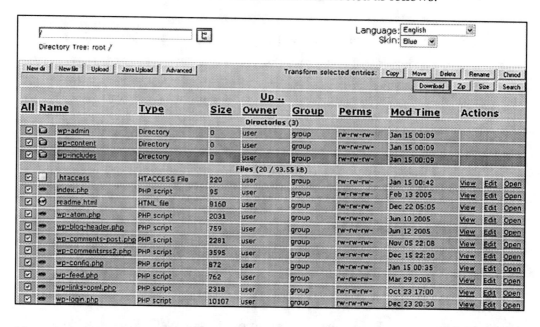

Now click on the **Download** button outlined. Then Net2FTP will make a ZIP file that contains all these selected files and download starts immediately. Save that file as a backup.

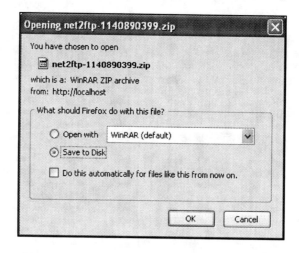

Backing Up Files Using Filezilla

Let's back up all these files using another famous and open-source FTP client, Filezilla. First create a folder where you will keep these files. Then log into your WordPress hosting account using Filezilla. After logging in, you will see all the files as shown in the following screen:

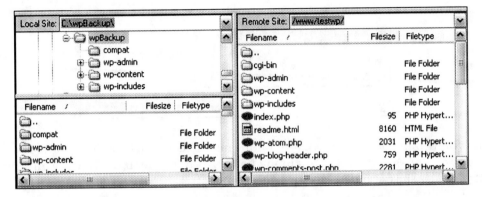

Select your backup folder in the left pane as highlighted in the preceding screenshot. Now select all files in the right pane. From here, it's just a kid's play. Drag these files from the right pane to the left pane. The file copy will start and you are done.

If backing up is successful, you can see all files downloaded to your backup folder that you had selected in the left pane.

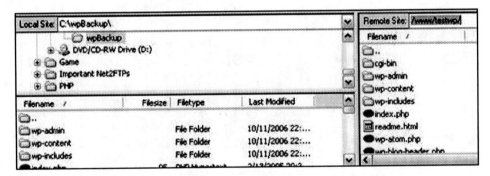

That's it! You have successfully backed up your WordPress files in your local backup folders.

Backing Up WordPress Database

You can use the popular and most available phpMyAdmin or any MySQL client to back up your WordPress database. Let us discuss the process of backing up.

Backing Up the Database Using phpMyAdmin

Firstly, log into phpMyAdmin. If you use the control panel, the URL of phpMyAdmin is `http://yourdomain:2082/3rdparty/phpMyAdmin/index.php`. After logging in, you can find the following menu on the right-hand pane of phpMyAdmin. From there, let us select **Databases** as highlighted in the following screen:

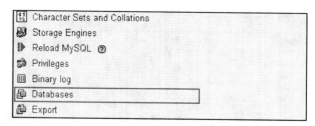

Now you will find all your databases on the next screen. Click on the database name that is used for WordPress. It will immediately open the database showing all your tables. Take a look at the following screenshot:

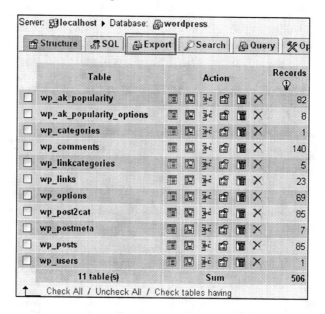

Please notice the **Export** button at the top of this page. Export is the process of saving your database in different forms. From phpMyAdmin, you can export your database into a plain SQL file, which you can run later on to retrieve the contents of your database. You can also export your database to a Microsoft Excel file, CSV (Comma Separated Value) file, XML file, and so on. For proper retrieval, we need to export this database into a plain SQL file.

Let us click on this **Export** button. You will be redirected to a page where you can select all the tables that you can export from this database.

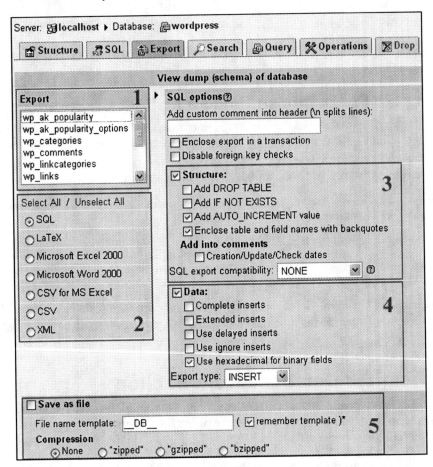

From the table names under the **Export** label, at the upper-left corner (the box marked **1**), you can select the tables to export. For backup, we must select all the tables. To select, click on the first table name, then hold down the *Shift* key and click on the last table name. All tables will be selected together.

From the section marked **2**, you can select the export format. This is by default set to **SQL** format. Keep it as it is. From the box marked **3**, you can select whether the structure of our database will be exported or not. From this section, check the first checkbox labeled **Add DROP TABLE**. This will generate an SQL command to drop the existing tables when you retrieve the backup.

From the section marked **4**, you can select whether the data of your database will be exported or not. From here, select the first checkbox labeled as **Complete inserts**.

This will generate a complete INSERT statement for every row in every table. From the section marked **5**, select **"zipped"**. Then, phpMyAdmin will compress the query inside a ZIP file. This is a suitable option because this SQL file is a plain text file and the compression ratio is quite high. This will save both time and bandwidth.

After downloading the ZIP file containing the SQL statements, keep it in a secure place.

Backing Up the Database Using a MySQL Command

You can back up your database using MySQL command tools. There is a tool named mysqldump, which is shipped with the MySQL default installation. If you have shell access and proper privilege, you can run this command in your server or from elsewhere. The structure of this command is shown as follows:

```
mysqldump --add-drop-table -h mysqlhost -u username -p databasename |
fileformat -c > filename
```

Here comes a real command:

```
mysqldump --add-drop-table -h phpxperts.net -u stanley -p phpxpert_wp |
bzip2 -c > phpxpert_wp.sql.bz2
```

After performing this command, mysqldump will prompt you for a password. If you provide the correct username and password, it will start downloading your database as an SQL file.

Restoring the Database from Backup

If anything goes wrong, you have to restore your database from the backup that we made earlier in this chapter. You can restore older files using FTP, but restoring the database needs some extra effort.

Let us see how we can restore our database using phpMyAdmin.

Restoring the Database Using phpMyAdmin

Log into phpMyAdmin, if you have it configured with your MySQL database, which you used for the WordPress installation. Select your WordPress database from the left pane. You should see all the tables in the right pane as seen in the following screenshot:

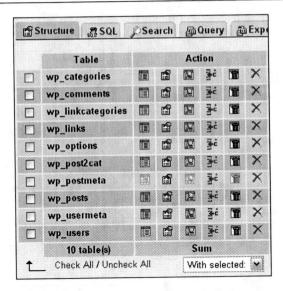

Check all the tables and from the drop-down labeled **With Selected** at the bottom, select the **Drop** option. You will get a page to confirm this deletion as follows:

Click **Yes** and the files will be deleted. Now your database is free from these corrupt tables.

Now you have to restore your database from the database backup, which you archived earlier. Extract the backup archive, and you will get a file with a .sql extension. For example, if the previous database name was wordpress, then the SQL file would be wordpress.sql. Now click on the **Import** tab from the top. You will get the following screen:

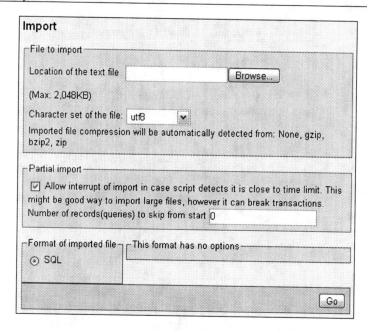

Browse the SQL file from your computer and click on **Go**. Immediately, it will upload the file and execute all the SQL commands stored in that file. If everything is OK, it will show that files have been imported successfully and you have successfully restored your database.

However, if you don't find any **Import** tab (for older versions of phpMyAdmin), then you have to execute the contents of the SQL file from the **SQL** tab. Click on the **SQL** tab at the top and you will get the following screen:

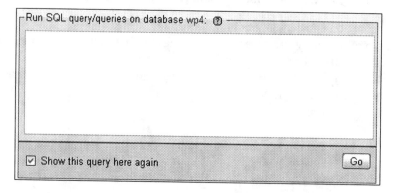

Open the SQL file using Notepad or any other editor and copy the contents from there. Paste the contents from the Notepad into this box and click on **Go**. If everything is OK, you will get a confirmation message on the next page that the

SQL queries have been executed successfully, which means you have successfully restored your old database.

Summary

WordPress is a famous blog engine, which is mature as well as popular. WordPress admin panel is designed to be very user friendly, the code is well structured for extension, and it can be extended by creating plug-ins. So your journey through WordPress is not finished, it's just the beginning.

We hope you have enjoyed this book and have got a strong base over blogging. Keep yourself in touch with this popular blog engine and the community. You will learn a lot of things by yourself and will enjoy using WordPress. Thanks again for your interest in WordPress and the open-source community.

Index

Thank you for buying
WordPress Complete

Packt Open Source Project Royalties

When we sell a book written on an Open Source project, we pay a royalty directly to that project. Therefore by purchasing WordPress Complete, Packt will have given some of the money received to the WordPress project.

In the long term, we see ourselves and you—customers and readers of our books—as part of the Open Source ecosystem, providing sustainable revenue for the projects we publish on. Our aim at Packt is to establish publishing royalties as an essential part of the service and support a business model that sustains Open Source.

If you're working with an Open Source project that you would like us to publish on, and subsequently pay royalties to, please get in touch with us.

Writing for Packt

We welcome all inquiries from people who are interested in authoring. Book proposals should be sent to authors@packtpub.com. If your book idea is still at an early stage and you would like to discuss it first before writing a formal book proposal, contact us; one of our commissioning editors will get in touch with you.

We're not just looking for published authors; if you have strong technical skills but no writing experience, our experienced editors can help you develop a writing career, or simply get some additional reward for your expertise.

About Packt Publishing

Packt, pronounced 'packed', published its first book "Mastering phpMyAdmin for Effective MySQL Management" in April 2004 and subsequently continued to specialize in publishing highly focused books on specific technologies and solutions.

Our books and publications share the experiences of your fellow IT professionals in adapting and customizing today's systems, applications, and frameworks. Our solution-based books give you the knowledge and power to customize the software and technologies you're using to get the job done. Packt books are more specific and less general than the IT books you have seen in the past. Our unique business model allows us to bring you more focused information, giving you more of what you need to know, and less of what you don't.

Packt is a modern, yet unique publishing company, which focuses on producing quality, cutting-edge books for communities of developers, administrators, and newbies alike. For more information, please visit our website: www.PacktPub.com.

Printed in the United States
94064LV00005B/23-40/A